Navajo

Facts On File, Inc.
460 Park Avenue South
New York NY 10016

Library of Congress Cataloging-in-Publication Data

Lindig, Wolfgang.
[Navajo. English]
Navajo / text, Wolfgang Lindig ; photos, Helga Teiwes.
p. cm.
Translated from the German.
Includes bibliographical references and index.
ISBN 0-8160-2756-0
1. Navajo Indians. I. Teiwes, Helga. II. Title.
E99.N3T3613 1993
979'.004972—dc20   92-42088

A British CIP catalogue record for this book is available from the British Library.

Facts On File books are available at special discounts when purchased in bulk quantities for businesses, associations, institutions or sales promotions. Please call our Special Sales Department in New York at 212/683-2244 (dial 800/322-8755 except in NY).

Book design by Heinz von Arx, Zürich (Switzerland)
Photolithography by Ast + Jakob AG, Köniz (Switzerland)
Translated by Barbara Fritzemeier and James Hulbert
Jacket design by Catherine Hyman
Composition by Catherine Hyman/Facts On File, Inc.
Manufactured by Mandarin Offset
Printed in Hong Kong

10 9 8 7 6 5 4 3 2 1

This book is printed on acid-free paper.

CONTENTS

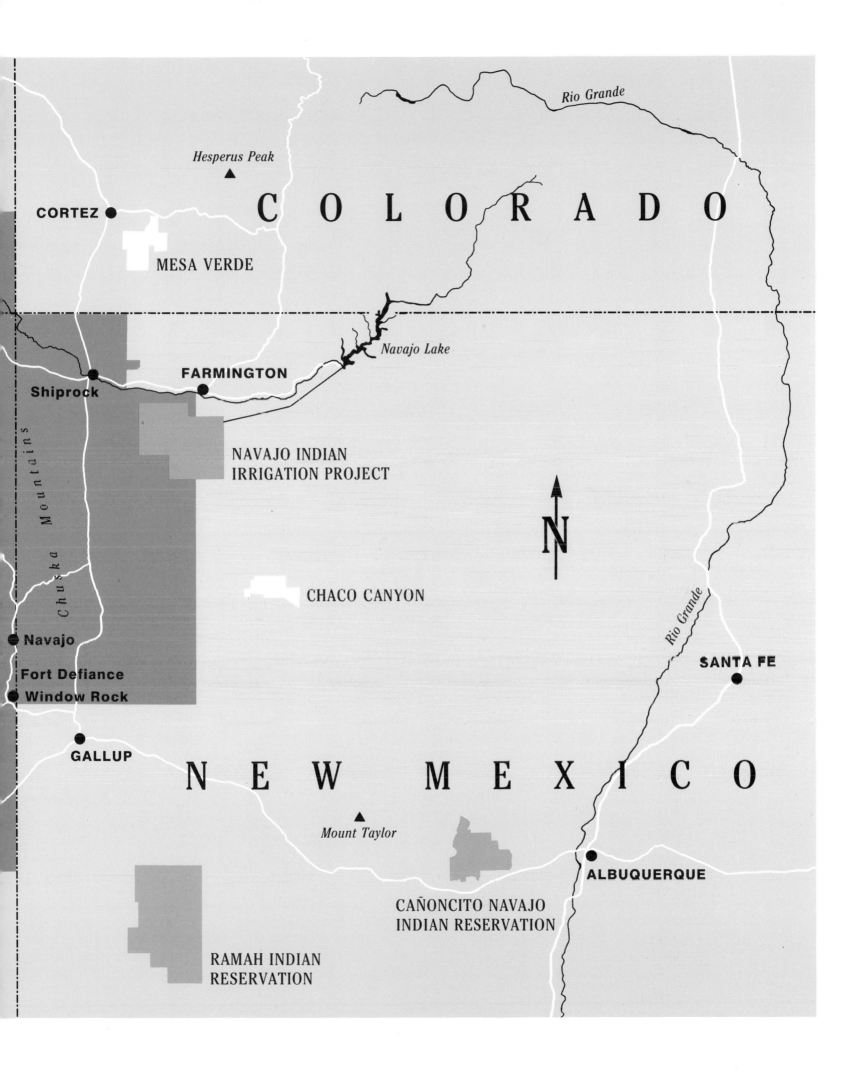

Hesperus Peak ▲

C O L O R A D O

CORTEZ ●

MESA VERDE

Rio Grande

Navajo Lake

FARMINGTON ●

Shiprock ●

NAVAJO INDIAN
IRRIGATION PROJECT

Chuska Mountains

N

CHACO CANYON

Rio Grande

● Navajo

Fort Defiance

Window Rock

SANTA FE ●

GALLUP ●

N E W   M E X I C O

Mount Taylor ▲

CAÑONCITO NAVAJO
INDIAN RESERVATION

ALBUQUERQUE ●

RAMAH INDIAN
RESERVATION

FOREWORD

Hozó   kehatíndo
In beauty, happiness   may (I) dwell

Hozógo   nasádo
In beauty   may I walk

Hozógo   sahatói   kehatíndo
In beauty   my male kindred   may (they) dwell

Hozógo   sezáni   kehatíndo
In beauty   my female kindred   may (they) dwell

Hozógo   sǐsikél   nahaltíndo
In beauty   my young men   may it rain on

Hozógo   sǐséke   nahaltíndo
In beauty   my young women   may it rain on

Hozógo   sǐnantáhi   nahaltíndo
In beauty   my chiefs   may it rain on

Hozógo   ní'yi   nahaltíndo
In beauty   us   may it rain on

Hozógo   ní'yi   nantádo
In beauty   (for) us   may corn grow

Tháditin   kehyetígi   nahaltíndo
Pollen   in the trail of   may it rain on

Ni'yitsǐ'dze   hozógo   nahaltíndo
Before us   in beauty   may it rain on

Ni'yikéde   hozógo   nahaltíndo
Behind us   in beauty   may it rain on

Ni'yiyá   hozógo   nahaltíndo
Below us   in beauty   may it rain on

Ni'yitsíga　　　hozógo　　　nahaltíndo
Above us　　　in beauty　　　may it rain on

Ni'yináde　　　dáltso　　　hozógo　　　nahaltíndo
Around us　　　all　　　in beauty　　　may it rain on

Hozógo　　　nasádo
In beauty　　　may I walk

Yúdi　　　sosádo
Soft goods　　　may I acquire

Ĭnklĭ'z　　　sosádo
Hard goods (jewels)　　　may I acquire

Lin　　　sosádo
Horses　　　may I acquire

Depé　　　sosádo
Sheep　　　may I acquire

Békasi　　　sosádo
Cattle　　　may I acquire

Sána　　　nagaí
In old age　　　wandering

Biké　　　hozó
Trail　　　beautiful

Nĭslíngo　　　nasádo
Lively　　　may I walk

from Matthews, *The Night Chant,
a Navajo Ceremony*

On behalf of the Navajo Nation, we express our best wishes for a successful journey through *Navajo*. The strength of the Dineh people comes from the knowledge of walking the Beauty Path in a harmonious manner. The photography in the pages ahead provides a glimpse into our world within the Sacred Mountains and under the Rainbow. May you share in this knowledge.

Vivian Arviso
Office of the President
Navajo Nation

ACKNOWLEDGMENTS

Helga Teiwes thanks the people and institutions listed below for the valuable assistance and support that she received while doing her work. She especially thanks the Navajos who allowed her to photograph them for this book.

Jan Bell, Chief Curator, Arizona State Museum, Tucson
Grace Ben, Lukachukai
Duane Beyal, Press Officer, Navajo Tribal Government, Window Rock
Gilbert Brown, Director, Office of Broadcast Service, Window Rock
Lucy Butler, Tuba City
Diane Dittemore, Curator of Ethnographic Collections, Arizona State Museum, Tucson
Linda B. Eaton, Curator, Museum of Northern Arizona, Flagstaff
Avyleni H. Greyeyes, Tuba City
Pete and Besse Greyeyes, Kayenta
Senator James Henderson, Jr., Window Rock
Wayne E. Hilgedick, Manager, Reclamation, Peabody Coal Company, Flagstaff
Larry Floyd Jackson, Monument Valley
Roy Lee Jackson, Monument Valley
Albert L. Keller, General Manager, Navajo Agricultural Products Industry, Farmington
Regina H. Lynch, Curriculum Coordinator, Rough Rock Demonstration School, Chinle
Bill Malone, Hubbell Trading Post, Ganado
Ed McCombs, Director of Public Relations, Navajo Community College, Tsaile
Wm. Bruce McGee, Keams Canyon Indian Arts, Holbrook
Kent McManis, Kaibab Shops, Tucson
Priscilla Neboyia, Chinle
Barbara Ornelas, Tucson
Silvano J. Perla, General Superintendent, Peabody Coal Company, Flagstaff

Edward S. Richards, General Manager, Navajo Forests Products Industries, Navajo
Carole Rosenblatt, Director, Artistic Galleries, Scottsdale
Dr. Raymond H. Thompson, Director, Arizona State Museum, Tucson
Dr. Gwinn R. Vivian, Associate Director, Arizona State Museum, Tucson
Ba'je Whitethorne, Flagstaff
Raymond and Colina Yazzie, Ganado

Wolfgang Lindig thanks especially:

Wolfgang Müller for careful editing of the text, especially for revision of the chapter on social organization;
Alfred Stolz for preparing the illustration depicting kinship structure;
Marianne Widmer, U. Bär Verlag, for support and encouragement in the planning and execution of the book.

THE ENVIRONMENT

A flat, barren high plateau dotted with occasional clusters of plant life—this is what Navajo country looks like to the casual observer. The people who live there call it Dinetah. Closer examination reveals the diversity and beauty of this magnificent landscape. Between 4,900 and 6,500 feet (1,500 to 2,000 meters) above sea level, the Southern Colorado Plateau lies on the border between Arizona and New Mexico. The plateau, enormous in scale, is broken up by mesas and innumerable canyons, washed out by runoff from the mesas. The Grand Canyon of the Colorado River, the largest of these "drainage ditches," cuts 5,900 feet (1,800 meters) deep into the underlying Paleozoic sedimentary stone and Proterozoic granite. This spectacular stratification, the result of deposits laid down by the forces of wind and water, has been opened to view as the river cut increasingly deeper due to geological forces acting on the plateau during the last million years. The Grand Canyon is located at the northwest edge of Navajo country. Its dimensions—217 miles (350 km) long and 17 miles (29 km) wide—exceed those of any other canyon on earth that was created by erosion. Other canyons, not as deep but still extraordinarily impressive, cut into the surface of the plateau; among them are Canyon de Chelly, Chaco Canyon, and the gooseneck meanders of the San Juan and the Little Colorado. In other areas it is not sharply etched gorges that characterize the country but the wide valleys and narrow mountain ranges of, for example, Monument Valley on the border between Arizona and Utah, where bizarre, wind-formed remnants of the plateau thrust upwards in the form of walls and pillars. Especially impressive creations of wind erosion are mushroom-shaped cliffs and the natural bridges and gates. The shimmering life forms of the Painted Desert, whose colors result from the multitude of alkalies and oxides that "bloom" out of the ground, seem to have been created by a painter's hand.

The country is accessible to humans only in the secluded valleys where water is available and where trees, shrubs and grasses grow. Numerous forms of wildlife are at home here, and this is where Native American people found shelter and settled. They lived in these places thousands of years ago, first erecting simple windbreaks, then building small houses sunk into the ground or cliff houses suspended under the overhanging rock. Later they built large towns. These first settlers were the Anasazi, ancestors of the Pueblo people who inhabited this land before the forebears of the Navajo migrated into the Southwest.

Upthrust formations and basalt peaks of volcanic origin form localized highlands that tower over the plateau to a height of 10,000 feet (3,000 meters). The most imposing of these are sacred mountains to the Navajo, protecting their land: to the west is Humphreys Peak, 12,667 feet (3,861 meters) high, in the San Francisco Mountains; to the north, Hesperus Peak, 13,221 feet (4,030 meters) high; to the east, Blanca Peak, 14,314 feet (4,363 meters) high; and to the south, Mount Taylor, rising to a height of 11,388 feet (3,471 meters). In contrast to the flat tablelands of the high plateau, these mountains and other mountain peaks and chains, such as the extensive Chuska Range and the Defiance Plateau, are wooded, and have served as the preferred hunting territory of the prehistoric and historic inhabitants of this land. Today they are used as summer pastures for the sheep and goat herds of the Navajo people.

Climate

Three zones determine the climatic conditions of the Colorado Plateau: (1) the wetter mountain regions, which comprise approximately 10% of the current area of the Navajo Reservation; (2) the moderate climate of the steppes—the mesas and high plateau that make up 30% of Navajo country; and (3) the relatively hot, arid desert of the low-lying land and valleys, comprising approximately 60% of the land.

The average annual rainfall fluctuates between 8 and 29 inches (20 and 75 cm). On the higher elevations and steep cliffs of the plateau of the western and southwestern territories, more rain may fall. During the summer, rain tends to occur in sudden violent cloudbursts. Since the parched soil cannot rapidly absorb the huge volume of water, this essential resource flows off into the arroyos that drain the mesas and funnel the runoff down into the canyons. The water is massed in the relatively few riverbeds, and flash floods are common. In the lower reaches of the Little Colorado, destructive flood levels

▲▼▲

several meters above the normal river level can be reached in a matter of hours. At higher elevations, a considerable portion of the annual precipitation falls as snow during the winter, sometimes remaining on the ground from November through April.

At this time of the year it is not uncommon for the temperature on the plateau to sink below −20°F (−30°C); in summer it can rise to 104°F (40°C). Spring is a season of persistent winds that tend to dry the surface soil. The sporadic rain that falls here evaporates rapidly, and the humidity is minimal. As a consequence, the air is almost always clear, and the high, snow-crowned tips of the volcanic peaks and summits of the Sangre de Cristo Range in northern New Mexico are visible at considerable distances.

Plant Life

Large forests in Navajo country occur only at elevations of at least 7,900 feet (2,400 meters) and consist of Ponderosa or yellow pine (*Pinus ponderosa*), Douglas fir (*Pseudotsuga menziesii*) and white oak (*Quercus gambelii*). At the warmer and drier lower elevations, occasional pinyon pine (*Pinus edulis*), juniper (*Juniperus* spp.) and live oak (*Quercus turbinella*) can be found. Once, trees followed the river valleys and formed small woods in the moist canyons. The old tree stands in Chaco Canyon were largely cut down by the Anasazi in the 12th century and have been replaced by junipers. Stands of cottonwood (*Populus* spp.) still exist along the arroyos and are occasionally found in the river valleys.

The remaining land, that which gives the region its essential character, is dominated by drought-resistant plant life well suited to the arid environment. Sparse sagebrush steppes consisting largely of *Artemisia tridentata* cover much of the high plateau areas; in the lower-lying zones the vegetation is dominated by yuccas (*Yucca* spp.), creosote bushes (*Larrea divaricata*), and mesquite (*Prosopis juliflora*). In the intermediate zone, at the base of eroded plateau escarpments, grow desert grasses essential to the grazing economy of the Navajo, among them Indian ricegrass (*Oryzopsis hymenoides*), sacaton grass (*Sporabolus* spp.), galleta grass (*Hilaria jamesi*), desert needle grass (*Stipa speciosa*) and chino grass (*Boutelona gracilis*).

Animal Life

Brown bears, wolves and deer once lived in the forests at higher elevations, and mountain lions, ocelots and beaver were indigenous to the river valleys. Although the animal population has been decimated by overhunting and the alterations made to the environment by commercial logging, mountain lions, lynx, black bear, blacktailed deer and bighorn sheep are still seen. Protected by the government, pronghorned antelope herds are again grazing on the steppes, particularly in Petrified Forest National Park. Small mammals such as jackrabbits, cottontail rabbits, skunks, gray fox, ferrets, coyotes and raccoons have been better able to adapt than larger animals. Although their populations are large, they are difficult to see because of their nocturnal habits. Birds are also abundantly represented; some of the larger species are golden eagles, redtailed hawks and other hawk species, turkeys, quail, screech owls and road runners.

Domesticated animals introduced by Europeans—sheep, goats, cattle and horses—are very visible, as are dogs, which were known to Native Americans thousands of years ago. The maintenance of extensive livestock herds, which have become the main source of food, risks overtaxing this delicately balanced environment. In the 1930s the United States government, in an effort to preserve the land, insisted on a drastic reduction of grazing herds. This proved to be catastrophic for the Navajo, psychologically as well as economically, since much of their outlook and life-style is dependent on the sheep herds.

On p. 15. Navajo horses in the northern part of the reservation, near the Utah border.

On pp. 16–17. Monument Valley, which the Navajo call Tse'bii'ndisgaii ("Valley of the Rocks").

Below. Ferguson Canyon in the western foothills of Navajo Mountain, with cottonwood trees.

Right. Sandstone weathering in Forbidden Canyon, west of Navajo Mountain.

Above. Wild larkspur. At an elevation of 6,000 feet, summer rains produce colorful displays of wildflowers.

Right. Cacti are found at lower elevations in Navajo country. They bloom in June.

On pp. 22–23. North of Kayenta, the 6,099-foot-high Agathla Peak, also called "El Capitán," towers over the plateau.

A cavity in sandstone, washed out by rainfall, holds seeds and spores, which can take root and grow here.

A pool of water in a rock cavity, several days after a summer rainfall. In the dry climate, these pools are often the only water supply on the elevated plateau.

On pp. 26–27. Wheatfield Lake, one of the few lakes in the Chuska Mountains, north of Window Rock. In the summer, this is a favorite spot for Navajos to visit.

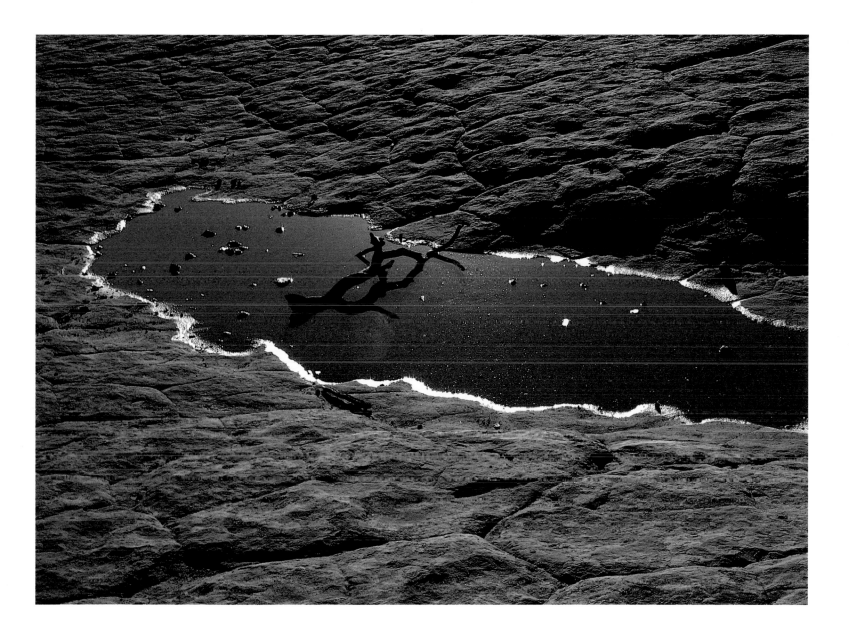

Below. Rainbow Bridge in Rainbow Bridge National Monument, Glen Canyon Recreational Area, is the largest natural stone bridge in the United States. It is sacred to the Navajo.

Right. The San Juan River in the lower part of Nasja Canyon, a few miles before it joins the Colorado.

Below. Rivers in the canyons freeze during long winter nights.

Right. Tsegi Canyon with its winter covering of snow. In this canyon are the famous ruins of Betatakin and Keet Seel.

On pp. 32–33. Canyon de Chelly, one of the most important agricultural areas for dry farming corn, beans and squash.

On p. 34. "This is how the white man imagines an Indian," says Larry Jackson, shown here in Monument Valley.

NAVAJO HISTORY TO 1850

The Migration South

Diné (the people) is what the Navajo call themselves in their own language. Until 1969, non-natives called these people "Navaho," the anglicized form of Navajo. The latter spelling is common today; the "j" is pronounced as an "h" and the emphasis is on the first syllable. The Spaniards, who borrowed the word Navahu, meaning "valley in which there are fields," from the Tewa language, placed the emphasis on the second syllable.

The Navajo speak a language that belongs to the Athapaskan language group. Since most Athapaskan languages are found in central Alaska and the inland areas of western Canada, there is no doubt that the ancestors of the southern Athapaskan people, Apaches and Navajos, at some time migrated south out of the western subarctic regions. It has been theorized that they separated from their northern (Athapaskan) relatives perhaps a thousand years ago to follow the Rocky Mountains south in small groups of hunters, gatherers and fishermen. Current research is undecided on whether these people stopped to establish communities on the plains (Dismal River Culture) as they moved south or whether they traversed the eastern part of the Great Basin.

The following observations can be made about the migration from the far north: It was not a concerted movement with any fixed destination; instead it had the character of a slow, steady expansion into new, sparsely inhabited regions, possibly the result of food shortages occasioned by a growing population. Further, the Rocky Mountains provided these nomads with ecological conditions similar to the subarctic homeland they had left behind. There appears to have been constant, if loose, contact among the bands that included even distant stragglers, insofar as they developed new survival techniques shared by all.

Separated from their North Athapaskan relatives, the south-moving Athapaskans developed a cultural inventory with certain distinctive characteristics. Basic foods were acquired by hunting, fishing and the gathering of wild plants, including berries, nuts and grass seeds. Hunting weapons were the

▲▼▲

bow and arrow and harpoons, and game was herded into temporary enclosures to be killed (chute-and-pound game drives). Tailored leather clothing with porcupine quill decorations was worn. Shelters were conical, tentlike structures—simple sapling frames covered with leather or bark. Shallow, coiled baskets were important utensils for the gathering of wild plants; pottery was unknown. Subarctic-type snowshoes provided mobility in snow. Dogs were utilized as pack animals. Religious practices were not systematized, although shamanism was practiced to enlist the aid of the deities in the hunt and to heal illnesses. Social organization was oriented around a flexible bilateral kinship system which, in practice, permitted a free choice of residence; clans did not exist. Political organization consisted simply of loosely structured bands. There was no institutionalized chiefdom; instead, temporary leaders were chosen to deal with unusual circumstances.

Arrival in the Southwest

It is assumed by historians familiar with southern Athapaskan cultures that these cultural characteristics were still largely in evidence when the Athapaskans first reached the Southwest. Only a few new elements had been adopted from other cultures with which they had made contact on the way; among these were familiarity with agriculture and pottery. It has been theorized that small bands living on the western plains may have joined the Athapaskans in their southern migration, or that survivors of the extinct Fremont Culture of the eastern Great Basin were integrated by the Athapaskans.

In approximately 1300 A.D. or shortly thereafter, the migration reached the periphery of Anasazi (ancient Pueblo) territory. Although no connection has been clearly proven, the possibility cannot be ruled out that the arrival of the Athapaskan hunters and gatherers caused the abandonment by the Anasazi of their northern communities.

Pueblos, Spaniards and Athapaskans

When the Spaniards pushed northward from Mexico into the northern Rio Grande Valley around 1540, they met with nomadic Native American people in the upper San Juan basin to whom they referred generally as "Querechos," or "Apaches." As of 1626 they differentiated between the northern Querechos of the Chama Valley and the upper San Juan basin and other Querechos/ Apaches because they had observed that the former practiced agriculture (corn, pumpkin, beans) and were able to utilize available resources rather efficiently. They called these people "Apaches de Nabajó." Their large population was attributed to these characteristics, and Spanish sources speak of them as a mighty tribe.

It is not, however, possible to identify the Apaches de Nabajó as being the same people as the historic Navajo, since the latter did not develop an ethnic identity until they had merged with Pueblo groups who fled from the Spaniards in the early 18th century.

The earliest descriptions of the Apaches de Nabajó are provided by the accounts of the Antonio de Espejo Expedition of 1582–83, followed by the chronicles written between 1630 and 1634 by the monk Alonso de Benavides, who lived in the region from 1625 to 1629. The Spanish began to settle New Mexico in 1598. They subjugated the Pueblo peoples, and Catholic priests established missions in their territory. Attempts at converting the Apaches failed; consequently the Athapaskans were not directly influenced by the Spanish. Apaches raided the Pueblo communities and Spanish ranches and, conversely, the Spaniards and allied armed Pueblos attacked the camps of the Apaches to provide slaves for their ranches and for their mines in Mexico There were, however, times when contacts between the various parties were peaceful. The Apaches de Nabajó traded meat, hides and mineral products, primarily salt and alum, to the Pueblos in exchange for cotton cloth, feather ornaments, horses, metal items and pottery. In the Pueblo villages they became familiar with such political positions as a wartime chieftain and a peacetime chieftain, and may occasionally have copied this system.

In 1680 the Pueblos united to revolt against their Spanish oppressors, and all soldiers, settlers and missionaries were driven out of New Mexico. Athapaskan bands participated in the revolt in revenge for Spanish campaigns into Athapaskan territory, as for example in 1678, when 50 Spanish soldiers and 400 allied Indians from Zia invaded Nabajó territory, plundering and burning settlements. Within a few years, however, Spanish troops were again advancing north from El Paso, conquering one Indian village after another despite occasional heavy resistance. By 1696 most Pueblos were under

Spanish rule again; only the distant Hopi villages in northern Arizona escaped being consistently occupied. Once the anti-Spaniard alliance of 1680 had been broken, the Pueblos ceased to resist the Spanish yoke. Thousands, however, fled to the territory of the Apaches de Nabajó on the upper San Juan River, north of the present city of Farmington. Since the Spaniards were consolidating their power along the Rio Grande and taking over areas west of that river, most of these Pueblo refugees apparently remained with the Nabajó. The cohabitation of these two peoples and the eventual blending of their cultures appear to have been the prerequisite for the emergence of a unique Navajo culture. It's been suggested that the merger of these two ethnic components was necessary to create the consciousness that has formed the modern Navajo identity.

It is difficult to establish this process archaeologically and ethnographically, as there is currently only sparse documentation and minimal evidence. Based on archaeological finds in the area of what is today Navajo Lake on the upper San Juan, the arrival of the migrating Athapaskans in the Southwest has been dated to 1300 A.D. The simple pottery found in this territory, the land called *Dinetah* ("Old Homeland") by contemporary Navajos, has been labeled "Dinetah Utility" by archaeologists. This type of pottery, dated to approximately 1700 A.D., was found together with Pueblo pottery. Under the influence of Pueblo potters, perhaps even inspired by prehistoric examples, a painted Navajo pottery called "Gobernador Polychrome" came into being. At the same time, pueblitos were being built—small multiroom structures with masonry walls, seemingly constructed for defense in many cases.

Archaeological excavations of village sites from the Dinetah after 1700 indicate that two different peoples lived here side by side: Athapaskans and Pueblos. The latter were sedentary and practiced agriculture, while the Athapaskans, mobile hunters and gatherers, lived sporadically along the San Juan. As the two peoples merged, the language and political organization, or local band structure, of the Athapaskans were preserved, while the concepts of the Pueblo people dominated religious and spiritual life. The Pueblos had, after all, rebelled against the Spanish primarily to resist religious oppression, and again resisted being forcibly Christianized after reoccupation by the Spanish in 1696. The numerous petroglyphs (rock art) of the Dinetah reflect the rich mythology, religious symbolism and highly developed ceremonial life of the Pueblos. Among the themes are found the hunchbacked god Kokopelli, depictions of shields decorated with sun symbols and macaw feathers, heart lines within animal figures, and scenic genres similar to prehistoric Kiva murals.

The new, distinct culture born out of this fusion, whose descendants we can now call "Navajo," came into being between 1710 and 1715 in the canyons of the dry river beds leading to the San Juan River: in Largo Canyon, Gobernador Canyon, Frances Canyon and LaJara Canyon, all of which lie south of the San Juan; and also in the river valleys of the Los Pinos and Animas, which flow into the San Juan from the north. This region has been thoroughly researched by archaeologists in recent years, providing an abundance of archaeological material documenting later developmental phases.

The small, easily defended villages situated on hills were characterized by the pueblitos, which usually consisted of one or several rooms with masonry walls and several small towers. Kivas, the round, semisubterranean ritual chambers found in Pueblo villages, are lacking; instead there are hogans, the house and ceremonial building form typical of the Athapaskan Navajo, consisting of a conical framework of logs covered with branches, sod or earth. The later-constructed pueblitos utilized ramparts, indicating the necessity of defending against raiding Utes, a neighboring tribe to the northeast.

The threat the aggressive and well-armed Utes represented was sufficient to cause the Navajo to leave the densely settled Dinetah around 1750 and move south into the Cebolleta Mountains and west into the Chuska Mountains, where they introduced other Southern Athapaskans, already settled there, to the "new culture." As numerous Spanish settlers, also fleeing the Utes, moved west, the old conflict between them and the Navajo was rekindled.

The Pueblo component of Navajo culture is visible not only in the masonry walls of houses and in religious practices, but also in small irrigation systems and the cultivation of cotton; in woven cotton clothing, tools for spinning and weaving; earthenware jugs, masks, tablitas (carved wood ceremonial head-dresses) and dried gourd ladles; cane arrow shafts, macaw images, sandals, close-coiled basketry, and the use of fireplaces as a means of drawing smoke from the interior of the houses. The most significant change, however, was the adoption of animal husbandry.

The significance of the sheep and goat herds of the Dinetah is disputed. Many of the Pueblo refugees had worked on Spanish ranches and had also kept their own animals, and brought their experience and knowledge of animal husbandry into the new culture. In 1786 the Spanish chronicler Pedro Garrido y Durán wrote: "Their possessions consist of 500 tame horses . . . approximately 700 black ewes, forty cows also with their bulls and calves. . . ." Goats are not mentioned, although they can be presumed to have been represented in large numbers, since goats must have been more at home in the rugged land of the Dinetah than sheep, and were an important source of meat and milk (even cheese-making had been introduced to the Navajo by the exiled Pueblos). After the Navajo withdrew from the Dinetah because of pressure exerted by the Utes, the cultivation of sheep took on more significance, and large herds developed quickly in the new territory. Around 1800 the Spanish governor, Don Fernando Chacón, wrote that the Navajo had countless flocks of sheep and also maintained cattle. It was at this time that the economy of the Navajo experienced a total change: These hunters and gatherers, who had learned to plant small crops on the side, were converted into passionate livestock breeders and herders.

Before touching on the consequences of this economic shift, it is important that we note that several Pueblo elements of social significance were also adopted, albeit in modified form. Among them is the organization of social groups into clans—large extended family systems of predominantly matrilineal character. The origin of the clans is extraordinarily complex. A number of clans can be traced back to old Athapaskan bands; others have their origins in group fragments of Pueblo refugees, in some of which it is possible to recognize existing Pueblo clans; still other clans can be traced to social groups that developed among captives, and even to combinations of the above.

The existence of a tribal council, called naachid, in the Dinetah is documented. The commonly used language that came to be accepted is Saad, the Athapaskan dialect, perhaps because the various dialects spoken by the Pueblo refugees were so different: some spoke Tewa, others Keresran, Zuni or Hopi—all of them mutually unintelligible.

As long as everyone coexisted peacefully and prospered in the fertile Dinetah, both the economy and the culture progressed, and the fusion of the Athapaskan and Pueblo peoples continued relatively undisturbed. As pressure from the outside increased, however, and an extended drought reduced the food supply of the rapidly growing population, latent tensions erupted. Since ancient times the Pueblo peoples had been deeply committed to their religion, engaging in complex ceremonies. These traditional beliefs had received a nativistic cast under the Spanish, but in the exigency of this contemporary crisis they reemerged. Restrained by Athapaskan values, the religious renaissance that occurred had bicultural features.

On the Athapaskan side, a different world order held sway, one that did not permit retreat into a religious shell. Connected as it was with the survival of a migratory people, it tended, in the face of a serious threat, to express itself more practically. The existential problems that had surfaced were best mastered by means of a mobile economy, such as the maintenance of livestock herds and intensive exploitation of local resources—indigenous plants and animals. The religious focal point of the Athapaskans is assumed to have been the "Blessing Way" (see page 174), which to a certain extent sanctions the life-style of Athapaskan society. It remains to be determined whether the Blessing Way ceremony was fully developed by this time or whether, inspired by Pueblo religious elements, it developed into the vital idea it later became.

The comprehensive changes that occurred contemporaneously with the departure from the Dinetah and the peaceful way of life there did not occur everywhere or uniformly. For example, although several of the groups that had resettled elsewhere continued to utilize the Pueblo building style, most Navajos returned to the simple, ancient house form, the hogan, because it was better suited to nomadic life. Between 1753 and 1770 many other such Athapaskan traditions reemerged, although Pueblo elements were still imprinted on the new culture. The end of this period coincided with the resumption of Spanish–Indian conflicts in 1774. Success in these skirmishes, characterized largely as running battles, undoubtedly contributed to a general acceptance of the young culture and the ideal canon it embodied. The extraordinary ability of the Navajo to adapt to new environments, their military response to the historic provocations of Spanish colonial power, the development of a flexible economic system with its tendency to increasingly large herds of livestock and to a higher degree of mobility, combined with the isolation of their territory, account for the strength and vitality of their society. Because the economic base was broad, the population rose steadily. This last factor contributed to the Navajos' increased military might.

▲▼▲

The Mexican Intermezzo

The period of Mexican rule in the Southwest was a relatively brief interlude. It was also a time of warfare. Many Navajos were captured and transported to Mexico, and internal factions formed within the tribe. A group called the "Enemy Navajo" (*Dine 'avia'i*) separated from their relatives in the hope of living in peace with white people, whom they accepted as an inevitable presence. This group later settled in the enclave of Cañoncito.

The Development of a Livestock Industry

The tremendous economic change that has come to define the national character of the Navajo, that still defines these people today, is the development of animal herds. The Navajo are the only North American Indian tribe that created a social and economic order based on the herding of domestic animals. Their values, intimately associated with the maintenance and development of their herds, resemble to an extraordinary degree the beliefs held by pastoral tribes in other parts of the world.

Beginning in the 1800s the Navajo were again capturing large numbers of animals in raids against Spanish settlements. Regular army units pursued the Indians deep into Navajo country. In 1805 a Spanish raiding party advanced as far as Canyon de Chelly, where soldiers killed 93 men and 25 women and children. The warfare between the Navajo and the Spanish, and as of 1821 the Mexicans, never entirely ceased. When the United States was at war with Mexico in 1846, the American military made a futile effort to protect its rear by making alliances with the Navajo. The failure of these treaties was foreseeable, since the Navajo had no centrally organized government and most village leaders did not feel obligated to honor treaties that had been entered into between the American military and other villages. The raids against Spanish and Anglo-American settlements continued. Between 1846 and 1850 the Navajo, in combination with Apache confederates, drove away approximately 450,000 sheep. In order to put a stop to the raids, the federal government established Fort Defiance in the heart of Navajo territory. When the fort had to be temporarily abandoned in 1861, during its tenth year, because its troops were needed to fight in the Civil War, New Mexico, according to a contemporary account, became a "madhouse": Navajos, Utes,

▲▼▲

Zunis, Apaches, Spanish-Americans and Anglo-Americans were in bitter conflict with one another. The bloodbath did not end until federal troops returned in 1863.

Despite the continuous conflicts directed against Spanish, Mexican, and Anglo-American settlements and army units, Navajo culture continued to stabilize. From the end of the 17th to the middle of the 18th century, it is estimated that there were 3,000 to 4,000 Navajos. Around 1850 the Navajo population is assumed to have been between 8,000 and 12,000. In other words, the population doubled in the first half of the nineteenth century.

Spanish reports dating from the second half of the 18th century document flocks of sheep consisting of several hundred animals each. Between 1846 and 1860, Anglo-Americans claimed to have seen hundreds of thousands of sheep. Actual counts were not possible, but it was estimated that the herds encompassed between 200,000 and 500,000 head. Even if one assumes these figures to be high, it is clear that Navajo sheep holdings increased considerably; increases in the number of goats, beef cattle and horses were not documented. On the other hand, in 1850 the herding economy alone would have been insufficient to ensure the survival of the Navajo people. Even if we accept the figures above, the ratio of people to domestic animals was 1 : 30. An efficiency factor of 1 : 40 or 1 : 50 is necessary to provide subsistence from livestock alone and to also guarantee the continuity of the herds. This means that, in addition to livestock, supplementary crops had to be planted whenever possible, and hunting and the gathering of wild plants continued to be essential, as they had been in earlier times. For this reason, it is debatable whether a livestock industry conducted by Native American people necessarily required raiding.

Navajo chief Narbona.

NARBONA
Head Chief of the Navajos.

Library, The Academy of Natural Sciences of Philadelphia.

NAVAJO HISTORY AFTER 1850

During a confrontation between the Navajo and United States troops on August 31, 1849 in the Chuska Mountains, Narbona Primero, an influential local Navajo leader, was killed. His death convinced even the friendliest Navajos that peaceful coexistence with whites would not be possible in the long run.

At this time white farmers and miners kept thousands of Native Americans, including many Navajos, as slaves. With a view toward assuring a continuous supply of cheap labor, it was in their interest to see the friction with the indigenous peoples continue. Tensions increased when white settlers drove their herds deep into Navajo territory. Protests to the responsible army officers proved fruitless. Under pressure from settlers in New Mexico, the land reserved for the Navajo was reduced, and this time the land reduction included agriculturally significant areas. The Indian agent for the Navajo realized the consequences of "depriving the best of the Indians of the grounds they cultivate and graze—whereon they raise corn and wheat enough to support the whole nation . . . thus forcing them either to violate the agreement forced upon them, or . . . to abandon cultivating the soil and stock raising or become pensioners on the government, or plunderers." A further reason for non-Indians to move into Navajo country was that it was suspected that gold, silver, and other valuable minerals could be found there.

Excluding brief periods when Indian agents and government officials managed the affairs of the Navajo responsibly, there were repeated violent clashes between the Indians and their American "protectors." In 1858 the conflict became so intense that Colonel Dixon Miles, with the support of the Commissioner of Indian Affairs, formally declared war on the Navajo. The warnings of New Mexico's civil governor and of several experienced officers were ignored. Enraged over the treatment they had received, more than 1,000 Navajos attacked Fort Defiance on the morning of April 30, 1860. Using largely bows and arrows—several ancient Spanish cannons proved generally worthless—they were almost successful in taking the fort. The Secretary of War subsequently ordered that regular federal troops move against the rebellious Navajo.

The Long Walk

In the fall of 1862, Brigadier General James Carleton arrived in Navajo country at the head of a large force of Union soldiers, the so-called "California Column." The War Department had sent him to New Mexico to defend the territory against invading Confederate troops. It was also his responsibility to prevent Indian raids against the overland mail route. After consultation with Henry Connelly, the governor of New Mexico, he ordered Colonel Christopher (Kit) Carson to pacify first the Mescalero Apache and then the Navajo. Carson, who had been an Indian agent, was not convinced that a military expedition against the Indians was necessary, but he followed orders. It took him only five months to overcome approximately 500 Mescalero Apaches and to have them deported to Fort Sumner (Bosque Redondo) on the Rio Pecos in New Mexico. In 1863 Carleton and Carson met with the leaders of a Navajo contingent seeking to avert war and convinced them that they too should move to Bosque Redondo. The uncompromising leaders, Barboncito and Delgadito, participated in the meeting but did not prevail. All Navajos who had not presented themselves at Bosque Redondo by July 20, 1863 were to be taken there by force by Carson and his second-in-command, the officer in charge of Fort Defiance. Most of the Navajos, living in their widely dispersed and isolated villages, never heard this ultimatum. Carson and his men began a campaign that would encompass most of Navajo country by the end of 1863, methodically destroying fields, orchards and villages, poisoning the water holes and slaughtering the livestock. The immediate cost of this scorched-earth policy was 301 Navajo dead, 87 wounded, 703 captives; the army reported 17 dead and 25 wounded.

Early in 1864, Carson and 375 men moved into Canyon de Chelly, the last stronghold of Navajo resistance. After only 16 days he returned to Fort Defiance, also known as Fort Canby, with 200 captives. Many of the Indians surrendered to the army because Kit Carson treated them well. In the meantime, other Navajos had also arrived at Fort Canby. On February 26, 1864, a prisoner detail left Los Pinos with 1,445 Indian people. In early March a second group of approximately 2,400 people followed, and on March 20th another 800. The "Long Walk," a trek of 300 miles (480 kilometers), was difficult at best. Those who could no longer walk were shot, including women and children; 323 people died in this way. Stragglers were attacked by white

Colonel Christopher ("Kit") Carson (left) and Brigadier General Carleton.

Photo by Nicolas Brown. Courtesy Museum of New Mexico, Neg. No. 9826.

settlers, who raided the small herds the Navajo had been allowed to take with them. Five thousand Indians had been anticipated, but in the end 9,000 Mescalero Apache and Navajo people found themselves crowded together at Bosque Redondo in March of 1864. A few people were successful in escaping back to their homeland, where they joined the free Navajos who had retreated into the lands south of the Grand Canyon and the Navajo Mountains, or into areas north of the San Juan and Colorado rivers, thus escaping deportation.

Conditions at Bosque Redondo were atrocious. The command at the camp had not counted on such large numbers. Lack of adequate shelter, blankets and clothing, and unfamiliar foods in quantities too small to prevent starvation, caused many deaths. Influential white citizens reacted to the unbearable conditions at Bosque Redondo by appealing to President Lincoln, to no avail. The martial law to which all Native Americans had been made subject, and which General Carleton in consultation with the war department had extended over New Mexico, made all overt actions futile. Many white Americans were outraged by the treatment of the imprisoned Indian people and actively supported their release. A judge and superintendent for Indian affairs in New Mexico lost their respective positions when they voiced their opposition. But the pressure of public opinion continued to intensify. It was convincingly argued that it would be far more practical for the government to send the Indians back to their homelands than to continue to feed them and their guards at a cost of more than a million dollars without noticeable improvement in conditions.

General Carleton was relieved of his command on September 19, 1866. In January 1867 the Bureau of Indian Affairs, now within the Department of the Interior rather than the War Department, assumed responsibility. In the meantime it had become obvious that a government plan to solve the food problem at Bosque Redondo by introducing agriculture was a failure, because of a plague of grasshoppers, water shortages and disease. In May 1868 a commission was sent to Bosque Redondo to investigate existing conditions and to determine whether the Indians held there could possibly be relocated in Texas or the Indian Territory of Oklahoma. Barboncito (*Hastiin Bidághaa'í*), the principal spokesman for the exiles, pleaded passionately that his people be allowed to return to their former homelands, which had proven to be relatively worthless to white interests and had remained largely unsettled. The members of the commission finally accepted Barboncito's plan and

▲▼▲

Top. Fort Sumner: Navajo quarters in Bosque Redondo.
Bottom. Command post of the military police. Navajos await the distribution of ration cards.

Both photos National Archives: U.S. Signal Corps coll.: III-SC-87965, III-SC-87966.

recommended to Congress that the Navajo be repatriated. Congress ratified the resulting treaty, and in the summer of 1868 the survivors returned to their homeland. It is noteworthy that this decision did not rest on humanitarian principles, but came about because the maintenance of the deported peoples was draining the national budget, which was already depleted after the Civil War. Imprisonment at Bosque Redondo had lasted four years, but the trauma suffered by the Navajo people is still visible today.

Return of the Exiles

More than 7,000 repatriated Navajos arrived at Fort Wingate east of Gallup in the summer of 1868. A horrendous sight awaited them—their fields were overgrown with weeds, the irrigation ditches filled with sand, the orchards destroyed; most families had lost all of their livestock. Many of those returning were forced to remain at Fort Wingate, and later at Fort Defiance, where they received food rations and blankets. Others attempted to find distant relatives or tried to survive by hunting and gathering wild plants. Since it was in the interests of both sides to avoid another Bosque Redondo, the Navajos' efforts to reestablish themselves received the support of the military. The army distributed sheep and goats as well as seeds for the next growing season, sometimes over the strong protests of white farmers. From the end of the 1880s until well into the 1890s, the Navajos lived peacefully under the protection of the American army. Their economy experienced a new upswing, once again they developed a high degree of economic independence; it was a period of near-prosperity.

The Reservation Period from 1868 to 1900

The new reservation, which assumed definite boundaries in the treaty of June 1, 1868, encompassed about 3,900 square miles (10,000 square kilometers) in the northwestern corner of New Mexico and the northeastern corner of Arizona. Certain places once inhabited by Navajos that had been important farming and grazing lands, such as the Chinle Valley, the Chaco Plateau, the Cebolleta and Zuni mountains, Black Mesa and the fertile region around Ganado and the valley of the Little Colorado River, were excluded from the original reservation. Between 1878 and 1900 the reservation was increased in size five times; by the turn of the century it had nearly reached its current size of 26,000 square miles (67,000 square kilometers; see the map on pages 4–5).

The new U.S. administrating body, the Navajo Agency, was first located at Fort Defiance but soon moved 37 miles (60 kilometers) to the southeast to Ojo del Oso, where the army could quash revolts from a safe distance. Maintaining bureaucratic control proved to be extremely difficult at the outset, particularly in view of the burgeoning population. By 1892 the Indian population had grown to approximately 18,000, with most Navajos living widely scattered in isolated and virtually inaccessible areas. Few Navajos spoke English. It was impossible for a single agency to overcome the transportation and communication problems, especially an agency that was physically distant from the reservation. Most of the agents, moreover, had no experience in dealing with Native American people, and given the many problems encountered in the performance of their duties, their tenures tended to be brief.

Traders

Government agents, preoccupied as they were with the survival of the Indian people, tended to play a subsidiary role in the organization of the reservation. The so-called traders assumed the more significant position of go-betweens, linking isolated Indian families and the outside world and acting as agents of cultural change. The traders were white men who settled near larger communities of Navajo people. Though "trader" is the established term, these men were not just businessmen. They had considerable influence on the lives of the Navajo people: They arbitrated conflicts within families and between unrelated groups; they introduced the Navajo to up-to-date technology by making the products of the industrial age available; and they purchased Navajo products such as blankets and silver jewelry, thereby contributing both to the perpetuation of a high-quality crafts industry and to the acceptance of Navajo craft items on the market. They also buried the dead, since Navajos fear the ghosts of the dead and had tended to burn deceased relatives along with everything they owned. Traders wrote letters for people and handled the mail. Beyond this, they acted as custodians of the family jewelry when Indian families went to the summer pastures, and also as pawnbrokers, holding jewelry against payment for goods on credit.

One of the first trading posts, Round Rock, established in 1885, was located in the heart of Navajo country. By 1900 there were seven trading posts and by 1910 the number had grown to 39. After that the development of trading-post networks stagnated because modern motorized transportation provided access to the distant white settlements with their varied and reasonably priced goods.

Cultural Change After 1868

The increase in the Navajo population to 20,000 by the year 1900 is phenomenal, considering the condition of these people upon their return from exile—a defeated people owning no more than they could carry. The dramatic transformation from desperate circumstances to renewed prosperity began not long after delivery of the first herd animals. Trade with the Anglos, which began with the trading posts, also contributed to the economic upswing. The construction of a railroad line south of the reservation provided jobs and, when completed, brought buyers for Indian crafts. The transportation network grew as roads were built and new means of travel introduced—first horses and wagons, later trucks and automobiles. Steel plows came into use. Government agencies began their work within the six newly created districts into which the enormous reservation had been divided. A health service was started and doctors were hired. Missions cropped up everywhere. The herds increased rapidly; estimates in 1892 put the number of sheep and goats at nearly one million.

No other phase in recent Navajo history illustrates more clearly the remarkable adaptive capacities of the Navajo people than the time immediately after their return from exile. During that same period many other Native American cultures collapsed.

On p. 53. The ruins of White House in Canyon de Chelly. The cliff dwelling was built by the Anasazi around A.D. 1100 and inhabited until 1275, long before the arrival of the Navajo.

On pp. 54–55. These petroglyphs in Canyon del Muerto represent mounted Spaniards; in the middle, wearing a black cape with a white cross, is a Franciscan monk. The drawing was done by Navajos around 1700.

Above. Tracking dinosaurs. A footprint in sandstone, millions of years old, is today a tourist attraction west of Tuba City.

Right. The ruins of Betatakin in Tsegi Canyon, to the west of Kayenta. This settlement, built into a large rock overhang, attests to the architectural abilities of the Anasazi who inhabited it around 1300.

Above. Gigantic natural stone chamber with a round opening to the sky in Monument Valley.

Right. The large petroglyph of an ox in Canyon del Muerto documents the reintroduction of cattle raising after the Navajos' exile to Bosque Redondo in 1868.

On pp. 60–61. An abandoned hogan, built in the old style with beams of pine arranged to form an approximately conical structure, the tips of the trunks protruding. The entrance once had a canopy, and the entire structure was covered with mud.

On pp. 62–63. The setting sun bathes the stone walls of the Manuelito Plateau in an intense reddish light. The plateau is situated above Black Creek Valley, north of Fort Defiance.

On pp. 64–65. Hubbell Trading Post, built by Juan Lorenzo Hubbell around 1883, is still in operation today near Ganado. It is protected as a historical monument, administered by the National Park Service.

Above and above right. Trading posts serve a variety of functions. For the Navajo, they are also pawnshops: valued possessions pawned there are usually redeemed if they are needed for ceremonies. Hubbell Trading Post Manager Bill Malone shows a large Ganado-style rug to a potential buyer.

Right. The historic Tuba City trading post.

On pp. 68–69. Main sales room of the Hubbell Trading Post. For more than 100 years, it has offered the Navajo everything they need in their daily lives.

Modern trading posts are tailored to car traffic: they are situated along well-traveled highways and can be quite large. The T & R Feed Company on Highway 666 in New Mexico caters to Navajos who stop here on the way back from Gallup (upper left) for propane for cooking, coal for heating, and feed for their animals. In Gallup, the closest major city to the reservation, Navajos shop on weekends and meet friends and relatives.

The T & R Feed Company also serves as
an automobile dealership.

TRADITIONAL ECONOMIC SYSTEMS

Animal Husbandry

The economic importance of herding in Navajo culture cannot be underestimated. Goats provided milk for dairy products, and since they are also a meat source, were a dietary staple. Sheep, on the other hand, were bred mainly for their wool. The trade in woven blankets, often called "rugs," was an important component of the tribal economy until the end of the 19th century, and as the price of wool rose, raw wool and mohair (the hair of the angora goat) were also marketed. Horses, mules and donkeys ranked immediately behind sheep and goats in terms of economic importance, providing transportation and, during severe winters, serving as a reserve meat source. Horses also figured in the status hierarchy; the more horses a Navajo owned, the higher was his standing in the community.

Beef cattle were of only minor importance during the early reservation period, and most animals were bred to be sold. It was considered an advantage that they required little attention.

Taking a broad view, it is possible to discern four phases in the development of the Navajo herds in the years from 1870 to 1900. At first the emphasis was on the breeding of many goats. This phase was followed almost immediately by an increase in the number of sheep. Third, the herding of the animals increased the need for horses and mules. Finally, as subsistence was assured and prosperity increased, beef cattle assumed a larger role.

Looking at this process in detail, it appears that at the time of their return from Bosque Redondo the Navajo had no more than 4,190 sheep and goats. The source of this figure is ferryman Santiago Hubbell, who ferried the homeward-bound families and their herds across the Rio Puerco and maintained records of the animals he transported. In November of 1868, under the terms of the treaty, the Indians received 1,000 goats (100 billy goats and 900 nanny goats) and 14,000 sheep (300 rams and 13,700 ewes). In addition, basic food items such as wheat flour and cornmeal, sides of beef, sugar and salt were delivered to them, so that at first it was not necessary to slaughter any

YEAR	SHEEP AND GOATS	CATTLE	HORSES	SHEEP UNITS
1868	4,190		1,570	
1870	17,300		8,000	
1871	30,000		8,000	
1872	100,000	6	10,000	
1873	175,000		10,000	
1874	125,000	1	10,080	
1876	400,000	1,000	15,200	
1878	500,000	1,500	20,225	
1879	700,000	1,600	23,000	
1880	700,000	500	41,500	
1881	1,000,000	800	40,500	
1883	1,000,000	200	40,050	
1884	1,000,000	300	35,075	
1886	1,100,000	1,050	253,500	
1887	1,050,000	2,000	245,000	
1889	900,000	5,000	251,500	
1891	1,583,754	9,000	118,798	
1894	1,250,000	1,200	100,500	
1900	401,882	6,858	38,260	
1904	754,500	12,100	65,626	
1912	1,461,776	30,290	330,000	
1914	1,687,726*	37,180	176,141	
1916	1,209,300	29,618	76,675	
1918	1,197,000	30,256	68,570	
1919	956,012	28,810	60,860	
1923	1,319,398	34,445	56,068	
1928	1,151,500	63,100	43,610	
1930	1,303,951	25,575	32,026	
1933	1,152,492			
1934	1,086,648			
1935	944,910			
1936	474,500	12,000	23,500	639,000
1937	436,757	17,380	38,159	702,072
1940	414,000	13,000	31,000	621,500
1945	316,000	7,000	26,000	477,000
1951	273,633	9,205	27,439	449,808
1960	390,767	15,482	20,680	556,095
1970	482,146	34,025	21,525	725,871
1975	510,301	47,524	28,949	845,142
**1988	197,300	42,000	11,700	

Condensed from Bailey and Bailey

* The number of donkeys (for this year) is included with the sheep and goats.

** These numbers are taken from the annual Navajo statistics "Fax" and do not include livestock from the Eastern District; therefore, the actual numbers may well be larger by one third than those shown here.

of the breeding stock. The number of animals increased considerably in the first years after the reservation was created, as a result of these factors and renewed raids undertaken by small groups of Navajo against the neighboring areas from 1868 to 1872. When the government made additional breeding stock available in 1878, especially sheep, such attacks decreased sharply.

The chart to the left illustrates the fluctuations of the herds since 1868. Although the figures may not always be exact, the chart does provide clearly discernible trends for different time periods. No dates are available for several years; the years from 1895 to 1899, for example, have been omitted. Where fluctuations in numbers are drastic, as was the case in 1872 and 1873, the lower figures are indicated in each column.

All statistics have to be considered in combination with continuing population growth and gradual increases in the size of the reservation. Between 1868 and 1930 the lands reserved for the Navajo increased from a round figure of 5,400 square miles (14,000 square kilometers) to 25,000 square miles (64,750 square kilometers); during the same period the population grew from 9,800 to 18,800. Because of an influx of Anglo-American cattle ranchers in the early 20th century, the government was unable to further extend the exterior boundaries of the reservation. The southern boundary was the railway from Albuquerque to Flagstaff, a 50-mile-wide swath that foreclosed expansion in that direction. The reservation consequently expanded to the west toward the Colorado River. To the east, Navajos and Anglos shared the pasturelands. In this area a checkerboard pattern of land ownership developed, with one farm in Indian ownership, the next in white hands. In 1882 the Hopis were given a reservation within the western part of the Navajo Reservation. An area used by both tribes, the Joint Use Area, has become a modern source of tension between the two tribes.

When the number of sheep and goats exceeded 1.5 million between 1891 and 1914 and no new grazing areas were available, the government decided to improve existing grasslands by constructing wells, dams and reservoirs. The program was only a qualified success. Since herds were reaching critical proportions, government agents warned that land erosion would occur. The Bureau of Indian Affairs, whether because of lack of funds or lack of interest, had done little to help broaden the economic base of the Navajo tribe by, for instance, promoting the use of more land for farming. The Navajo themselves showed little inclination to farm, preferring to sell or barter their stock and animal products, especially wool, to the traders in exchange for wheat flour and other food staples, and they continued to buy corn from the nearby Hopis or Zunis.

The slow but steady transformation of the Navajo economy was also influenced by outside forces that all tended to be associated with the flood of Anglo-American goods that had become available. When the Atlantic and Pacific Railroad was extended from Albuquerque to Gallup in 1892, the amount of wool exported, which had been negligible up to that point, rapidly increased to 1,100,000 pounds (500,000 kilograms) annually. Since livestock could be transported relatively conveniently and cheaply by train, cattle ranching became more attractive. The traders, who were by this time represented in larger numbers, also encouraged commerce by offering credit. Attractive products offered on credit increased the dependency of Indian people and led to a benign sort of indenturing. As a result of growing competition among themselves, the traders themselves came under pressure from wholesalers. These forces worked together to form a vicious circle: The Navajo had to produce more in order to maintain their standard of living in the face of a growing population and rapidly deteriorating conditions of production, such as reduced soil quality, the catastrophic drought of 1893/94, and the severe winter of 1894/95. To make matters worse, the nationwide recession of 1893 caused the bottom to drop out of the market for livestock and wool. This combination of factors rapidly altered the economic position of the Navajo. Intensive herding left little room for flexibility in adaptation, and consequently the old form of economic management collapsed, and with it disappeared the temporary prosperity of the Navajo people.

Animal Ownership and Breeding During the Transition

The number of goats and sheep a family keeps is not only a measure of prosperity but reflects a vital aspect of Navajo cultural identity. The herds assume a position in the Navajo mind that is difficult for non-Indians to comprehend. For this reason, problems with the breeding and keeping of herd animals in recent Navajo history deserve attention, as do the resolutions of these problems within the context of Navajo history and the limitations of the reservation environment.

At the turn of the century the Navajo owned 400,000 goats and sheep, which is fewer than before 1893 and more than during the herd reduction of the mid-1890s. The herds had apparently recovered by 1900. In 1915 nearly two million animals were again grazing on Navajo land. This increase is due partly to improvements in animal husbandry, and partly to the restriction on sales of animals imposed by the government after 1900. In order to meet the national need for meat, restrictions were lifted during World War I and the number of animals dropped to under a million by 1919 because of favorable prices and good sales. Marketing difficulties brought on by inflation, and the less-than-successful regulatory measures then used by the Navajos to control sheep populations, soon drove the numbers up again.

The Navajos traditionally kept the rams with the herds year-round, and no "lambing season" existed on the reservation. In the winters the mortality rate among lambs was high and the lambs that were born tended to be weaker; consequently it was difficult to sell them the following fall, and many had to be slaughtered. Such losses were avoided by controlled breeding. At first, leather "aprons" were tied around the bellies of the rams; later the rams were simply separated from the rest of the herd. It was nearly a decade before these methods were accepted in all of Navajo country.

In order to improve the quality of wool produced by the Andalusian churro sheep introduced by the Spanish in 1598, and long since inbred, merino rams were introduced as early as the 1880s, and later Rambouillet rams were brought in to broaden the available gene pool. Initially the Navajo did not support these experiments. However, once it had been shown that the wool of the newer varieties of sheep found a readier market than the wool of the hardier churro sheep, they recognized the necessity of improving the stock.

Navajo goats are descended from common Spanish milk goats. Increasingly conscious of the market, the Navajo began breeding Angora goats with these native goats at the beginning of the 20th century. The resultant fine mohair wool proved to be a saleable product, and the new crossbred goats were not slaughtered. The decision to breed goats to maximize wool production was made at a cost, because this new type of goat produced less milk. In order to maximize both wool and milk production, Angora goats were bred together with Toggenberg goats. In the 1930s, mohair prices fell drastically because the railroad companies, which had previously upholstered their train seats with mohair, stopped ordering wool. The number of goats on the reservation was consequently greatly reduced.

The cattle industry developed in a direction almost diametrically opposed to that of sheep and goat herds. The cattle herds grew rapidly, from 1,658 head in 1900 to 37,180 in 1914, shrank to 29,310 in 1915, and then stabilized at that level. At the turn of the century, Navajos owned primarily Mexican or Texas longhorn cattle. Until the 1920s the Navajo considered them an inferior meat source. After Hereford bulls were brought in to stud, however, the quality of the meat improved so much that Navajo beef was able to compete on the American market.

The trend to solid ungulates (horses, mules, donkeys) followed yet another course. In 1904 the Navajo owned approximately 65,000 horses; in 1912 the number was estimated at 330,000. During World War I the number of horses was reduced considerably, due to disease, eventually stabilizing at 60,000.

The Stock Reduction Program

The economic independence of the Navajo ended in 1933 with direct Bureau of Indian Affairs (BIA) intervention into the management of the herds. The herds were to be reduced by 1936, initially on a voluntary basis. If the reduction proceeded on a voluntary basis, the government would compensate for the losses by increasing the size of the reservation, constructing irrigation projects, and developing the infrastructure; the jobs created by these projects would be a desirable byproduct. This promise, made in good faith by then-Commissioner of Indian Affairs John Collier, was never approved by Congress. Because this occurred during the Depression, the government instead bought livestock at low prices to feed the hungry unemployed in the eastern states. When the transportation system failed in the confusion brought about by the economic collapse, purchased animals were slaughtered before they reached their destination and the meat was either distributed or burned at the train depots—something the Navajo have never forgotten.

The U.S. government began systematic livestock reduction in 1936; the process was to be completed by 1941. The reservation was divided into 18

▲▼▲

Grazing Districts, also called Land Management Units, and the livestock-carrying capacity of each unit was estimated. If the livestock exceeded the predetermined grazing capacity of the pasture, which was measured in "sheep units" (one goat = one sheep, one cow = four sheep, one horse = five sheep) and worked out in set quotas, the animals in excess of the quotas were cut out. According to regulations in force at that time, a herd could only be increased by permit, and since these permits were issued only to the pasture of a given community, the mobility of the herds was affected. Animals could not, for instance, be moved onto the grazing lands of relatives, even if their pastures were located within the same "unit" and were not in use. The herding cycle and social system connected to seasonal changes in grazing lands, necessary for survival in an area where land is so unevenly productive, was interrupted by the newly enforced system.

The forced reduction of the herds, which led to a 65% loss of Navajo livestock, has been the most decisive event in Navajo history since the Bosque Redondo captivity. In the eyes of the Navajo it was not solely a question of protecting the ecosystem—they were in essential agreement that this was necessary—but it constituted a significant and sudden interference with the social frame of reference associated with the herding system. The dignity of individual Navajos was threatened.

History from 1950

The Navajo were increasingly forced to seek other sources of income. The primary source was welfare payments made by the state; a secondary source was within and without the borders of the reservation. During World War II many Navajos were drafted or worked in war-related industries, temporarily camouflaging the need for jobs. The situation worsened with renewed reliance on local resources as the war drew to a close. The Navajo-Hopi Rehabilitation Act of 1950 prevented a catastrophe by making $80 million in aid available. It was obvious to the government and to responsible BIA personnel that temporary programs, like those provided to other Indian tribes, failed to solve the chronic, underlying problems of the Navajo, although they did provide a quick fix. Apparently, the plan behind such half-hearted measures was the eventual dissolution of Indian reservations through the Termination Act—the termination of federal benefits and services and the forced dissolution of the reservations into privately held lots. The Relocation Program, which encouraged the resettlement of Native American people in urban centers, was part of the termination policy. Many Indians, attracted by the premiums paid to those who relocated, did move to the cities; however, few ever found employment. Since the Navajo as a people never relinquished their claim to the land, a termination act specifically terminating their reservation or their tribal standing was never enacted.

The livestock business did recover in these changed economic circumstances: The narrowly drawn regulations regarding the issuance of grazing permits were loosened considerably. In 1956 the Tribal Council, the Navajo's governing body, assumed authority over all issues relating to the pasturing of animals. The guidelines established in 1937 regulating the number of animals that could be grazed were largely ignored and, by 1974, the herds were again as large as they had been before the forced reduction: approximately 900,000 sheep units.

The BIA and tribal planners today view the herding and breeding of stock animals as a relatively minor part of the tribal economy. Market prices tend to be rather low, and the Navajo themselves consume increasingly fewer of their own products, including meat. Each family nonetheless takes pride in the maintenance of a small herd, considering fresh meat to be superior to the frozen products available in supermarkets. The maintenance of herd animals continues to be a long-term capital investment valuable to the people.

The rangeland, on the whole, looks better today than ever before. There are more water sources, meadows are being resown and often fenced as well. In many parts of the reservation feed is being produced at levels two to four times higher than had been the case; consequently, more animals can be maintained on the same amount of land. The tribal government has independently financed the digging of wells and, when shortages occur, it transports feed and water to the suffering animals. In the early 1970s the Tribal Council created a self-help organization to purchase wool and market livestock to cut out middlemen. This has helped to stabilize fluctuating wool prices.

The size and composition of the herds has nonetheless changed considerably between 1951 and 1975. The number of sheep and goats rose until 1965 and has remained constant since then. Beef cattle herds have been growing steadily since 1950. This is indicative of a radical change in the economic situation of the Navajo: Since most Navajo people now depend on jobs for a living, they have less time to care for their goats and sheep. Beef cattle, on the other hand, do not require constant attention. This shift in the comparative value of different stock animals is also reflected in the trade balance of 1987. The tribe sold 60,000 sheep, 25,000 goats, 40,000 head of cattle, and 5,000 horses at a combined value of approximately $20 million; beef cattle were responsible for the largest part of that income, about 80%.

Agriculture

Compared to herding, agriculture plays a subsidiary role for the Navajo people. Historically, it was the Pueblos who introduced sophisticated farming techniques into the shared community, while the Athapaskans mainly exhausted the natural resources of an area before turning their efforts increasingly to animal husbandry. But even these people had on their southward migration become familiar with the cultivation of plants and had seen planted fields, albeit in modest proportions. Apart from small "kitchen gardens," the possibilities for extensive farming are extremely limited in Navajo country, where there simply is not enough water. Permanent fields are possible only on a few strips of land where rain falls in adequate quantities. Even on these narrow strips, the fields had historically tended to be small, and they were neglected when the time came to move the herds to summer pastures at higher elevations. At these elevations, in turn, the long cold season prevented the planting of fields. Consequently, one finds Navajo fields either widely scattered in the few river valleys, for instance along the San Juan, or in the canyons where water supplies are adequate during the summers. Frost is not as common here, making it possible for the crops, particularly corn, to ripen. It has been these areas which Native American people have historically been forced to relinquish to white farmers.

As early as 1865 the decision was made to concentrate the Navajo within agricultural "farming pueblos." Government agents favored farming as a means of survival because, compared to ranching, it required a smaller land base. An additional consideration was that it would facilitate the control and administration of the tribe if they were concentrated in villages. Those promoting this plan believed optimistically, and incorrectly, that the Navajo had learned the basics of agriculture at Bosque Redondo. In view of this misreading of the realities, the treaty of 1868 furthered agricultural development by allocating far more money for that purpose than for livestock. For ten years, from 1869 to 1879, the Indian agency distributed seeds and farming equipment to Native American people free of charge; after that the acquisition of these items was to be financed by other sources.

It was anticipated that corn and wheat would be planted in equal proportions. The Navajo had been growing wheat on a limited basis since the beginning of the 18th century, much as they had been planting corn since that time—a grain they generally preferred to wheat. They would plant several kernels together on widely spaced mounds, a system intended to preserve the soil. Beans (long known to the Navajo), watermelons and pumpkins were planted alongside each other. Now turnips, beets, cabbage, peas, sweet potatoes, carrots, onions, cucumbers, tomatoes, sugar beets, spinach, cauliflower, asparagus and potatoes were offered as possibilities. Despite the varied offerings, only potatoes came to be of any importance.

Since the Navajo were not moved to devote greater effort to farming even in view of the broad spectrum of produce available to them, the gifts of hoes, spades, sickles, rakes, axes, shovels and pickaxes proved likewise uninspiring. A simple digging stick continued to suffice for the planting of corn. Only plows were considered desirable and were put to actual use in the larger fields within irrigation districts.

To irrigate their fields, the Navajo dug canals for the snowmelt water that ran off from the nearby mesas and directed it to the fields, an often difficult process. When this inefficient method was used, even the sowing of seeds was dependent on the anticipated water supply that would, depending on the snowfall, be available in spring. The intensity of agricultural activity was, therefore, a matter of climatic conditions rather than economic need. It is another indication of the Navajos' lack of interest in farming, much less in the development of the agricultural potential of the land. With the increased importance of herding, the role of farming was further diminished. Cosmos Mindeleff, an anthropologist active in the Southwest, wrote in 1898: "The people who live here [in Canyon de Chelly] are regarded by other Navajo as poor because they own but few sheep and horses and depend principally on horticulture for their subsistence."

The United States government did everything in its power to help the fledgling agricultural economy to grow. In 1894 American engineers constructed Cambridge Ditch in the San Juan Valley, a state-of-the-art irrigation system, which at first only irrigated a parcel of three square kilometers. Although the system was expanded, most Navajos in the area continued to utilize their old, inefficient methods. It was not until 1899, under the guidance of S. E. Shoemaker, the "Head Farmer for the Navajo Reservation," that the system was expanded in the area near Fruitland, to encompass nearly 5 square miles (12 square kilometers). In 1910/11, Cambridge, now called Hogback Ditch, served an area of 8 square miles (20 square kilometers). Most of the work was done by hand, with small hoes; modern tools were not available to the Navajo.

By the 1920s most of the Indian people along the San Juan owned plows and harnesses. An agricultural research facility familiarized them with new crops. The planting of alfalfa as winter feed proved to be a successful venture. The Shiprock Agency, established in 1903, furthered the development of peach, apple, cherry and plum orchards.

Outside the San Juan Valley area, agricultural programs existed only in the vicinity of Fort Defiance, at Ganado, and near Marsh Pass in western Navajo territory. Experiments begun in other places were soon discontinued. Nonetheless, the cultivation of potatoes took hold in the eastern part of the reservation. On the rest of the reservation, crops were not produced in amounts sufficient to meet subsistence needs.

Despite all efforts to create an effective farming economy on Navajo lands, attempts at agriculture remained fruitless. In the 1950s, the Navajo Indian Irrigation Project (NIIP), an ambitious undertaking intended to work in conjunction with the San Juan-Chama Diversion Project, built a series of dams, tunnels and diversion channels through the Continental Divide, making it possible to divert water from the San Juan River basin to the Rio Grande basin. With the consent of the tribe, construction of the Navajo Reservoir on the San Juan began. It guaranteed the tribe a water supply of 508,000 acre-feet (or 626 million cubic meters) annually. It was foreseen that water from the reservoir would irrigate 173 square miles (448 square kilometers) by means of 11 pumping plants. It was also anticipated that the project would create 20,000 jobs, with an additional 16,000 jobs resulting from the projected agricultural development. Ground for the Navajo Dam was broken in 1964, but the first pumping plant, which irrigated 15 square miles (40 square kilometers), did not go into operation until 1976.

The water in the reservoir, called Navajo Lake, was originally intended to irrigate farms held by individual families. After careful consideration, however, the Tribal Council decided to create a tribal enterprise, the Navajo Agricultural Projects Industry (NAPI). Experimental farms near Farmington and in the Fruitland area under the Council's leadership have been a great help to Navajo farmers.

In 1990 six of the Navajo Indian Irrigation Project's pumping plants were in operation, and the seventh was to begin pumping in 1991. The 72 square miles (187 square kilometers) of arable land this created, predominantly under the authority of the NIIP, produced a profit in 1987. Broken down by crops into percentages, production was as follows: 24% beans, 19% corn, 14% alfalfa, 8% potatoes, 5% winter wheat, 3% barley; the balance was fallow land.

The annual report of the Navajo Economic Development Program released by the Navajo Tribe in Window Rock in September 1988 provides an overly optimistic projection for future development of the irrigation project. In view of continued resistance to farming, and the financial problems that still trouble the NIIP, a cautiously neutral view might show the current projections to be wishful thinking, rather than a realistic estimate of what can actually be achieved.

Subsistence Economy (Hunting and Gathering of Wild Plants)

Early Spanish chronicles describe the Apaches de Nabajó as passionate hunters and their native territory, the Dinetah, as providing excellent hunting opportunities. It is indicative of the prominent place that hunting assumed in the life of Navajo forebears, a passion undoubtedly brought along from the northern taiga, that these people staged communal hunts in which parties of men would leave their riverine villages for days at a time.

Like all hunters of wild animals, these Athapaskans felt a kinship with certain species of animals. In order to appease the violent death of these "relatives," or to prevent the victim from taking revenge on the hunter, certain ceremonies had to be fulfilled. The rituals performed before, during and after

▲▼▲

a hunt (*dini'ee*) served the Navajo as a prayer for forgiveness. This sort of appeasement was not required for all animals. Anthropologist W. W. Hill observed that blacktailed deer, pronghorn antelopes, brown bears and golden eagles were ritually hunted. Wrote Hill in 1938:

> The ritual behavior and observances employed were of the same pattern as those used in the chants and in war. The hunting party was under the direction of a shaman or chanter. This man instructed the hunters as to their conduct, and performed and directed the rituals.

Other animals such as mule deer, bighorn sheep, mountain lions, badgers, martens, beaver, otter, turkeys and sage hens were killed whenever they were encountered. The Navajo sometimes drove animals into previously constructed enclosures or traps. Other hunting methods and tricks were also employed, such as sneaking up to the game in an animal disguise.

In the decade following the return from Bosque Redondo, when the domestic herds were still small and it was necessary to preserve domestic breeding stock rather than to slaughter these animals, the Navajo people depended much on game. The indigenous wild animal population had increased considerably during the long absence of the Navajo. Conversely, now that they were heavily hunted, the population of game animals dropped rapidly. By 1876, within just eight years, Navajo and Ute hunters eradicated virtually all wild animals from the San Juan Valley. This overkill was most likely due to the fact that the Navajo, once limited to bows and arrows, spears, traps and nets, now hunted with rifles from the backs of horses, which broadened their hunting areas and generally improved their chances of a kill. Several additional factors, among them competition from grazing herds or diseases such as mange, hastened the decline of the pronghorn herds. By the mid-1880s the most significant game animals had disappeared from Navajo territory. It was, therefore, necessary to extend hunts to increasingly distant places, such as the Colorado Rocky Mountains.

Even after the eventual increase in domestic herds, now capable of satisfying the need for meat, the Navajo continued to hunt. The hunt was no longer conducted for survival but primarily for skins and furs to make moccasins, and for trading purposes. Since the large game animals, deer and pronghorn antelopes, were rarely found anymore, the Navajo suffered a

▲▼▲

shortage of hides and actually traded wool for the skins of wild animals. Even cowhides were now used.

Prior to the introduction of domestic herd animals and agriculture, the gathering of wild plants played a role comparable to that of hunting in the subsistence economy of the Navajo people. Even later, especially in times of shortages, as after 1868, the Navajo still returned to this source. They utilized primarily the nutlike kernels of the pinyon (or piñon) pine, acorns, walnuts, sunflower seeds, mesquite beans, wild potatoes, the fruit of several types of cacti, grass seeds and other grains, and the fleshy leaves of the agave plant or the spinachlike leaves of the goosefoot. Since the fruit and other usable parts of plants ripened or matured at different times, seasonal gathering expeditions had to be undertaken, on which a number of specialized receptacles and tools were essential, such as baskets, sieves, picking devices and tongs for the harvesting of cactus fruits, and threshing devices for removing the hulls from grass seed, among others. Beginning in the 1920s, pinyon nuts began to assume economic importance as an item of commercial value beyond the boundaries of the reservation. In 1926 the sale of pinyon nuts from the Southern District brought in $420,000.

Horses are the pride of the Navajo man. Sheep, goats, and cattle belong to a wife, but horses are always exclusively the property of the husband. Even today, if a couple divorces, the man gets horse and saddle, the woman everything else.

For the Navajo, however, horses do not represent merely prestige and property; there is a close relationship between human and animal. In fact, the Navajo man's horse is shot when its owner dies, so that the soul of the dead man can continue to ride with the soul of his horse in the other world.

Before the automobile, the horse was the most important means of transportation. Even today, it is extremely important in farm work, hunting, and especially for herding sheep and cattle. Horses are also used in the springtime cattle drive to the cooler mountain regions and on their return to the valley in the fall.

Here eight horses traverse the Tsegi Canyon.

On pp. 88–89. Horses in the vast valleys of Monument Valley.

On pp. 90–91. Despite the sparsity of vegetation in the less elevated parts of the reservation, the Navajo are successful cattle ranchers. Wind-driven pumps are used to gather drinking water in tanks for the herds. Here Navajo cowboys are watering their horses.

Navajo cowboys lassoing cattle. Every spring the young cattle chosen for breeding are branded to show who owns them; the others are sold.

Severe winters make harsh demands on humans and animals. At high elevations, snow remains on the ground for months at a time, and the temperature can fall below −20°F. Horses, sheep and goats are driven out even in the snow and

cold onto the near-barren pasture to seek sustenance. It usually turns out, however, that they must additionally be fed hay and alfalfa as fodder.

On pp. 96–97. A small herd of sheep in Monument Valley is driven homeward.

Roy Lee Jackson with one of his four-horned rams. These animals—few of which are extant today—still exhibit traits of the churro sheep that Spanish settlers brought from Mexico in the 16th century.

Right. With her grandson's help, Besse Greyeyes drives her sheep and goats homeward from the Tsegi Canyon.

On pp. 100–101. The brothers Larry and Roy Lee Jackson drive their herd down a sand dune, toward a creek, to provide water for the animals.

On pp. 102–03. Vegetation is so sparse that herds must change pasture often.

Below. Children take on responsibilities when they are still very young. They watch the herds and take special care of the young animals.

Top right. Besse Greyeyes at her daily work with the animals: fetching water (her house has no running water), bringing lambs to their mothers to nurse, preparing food for the sheep dogs, and much more.

Right. When not grazing, the herds stay in a corral near the house.

On pp. 106–07. A large herd of sheep and goats pass between sandstone formations in Monument Valley.

Top. Since the farmland belongs to the women, it is their responsibility to cultivate it. Besse Greyeyes holds squash seeds in her hand before planting them.

Bottom. Kernels of corn for planting are placed in an indentation below the surface; then earth is spaded over them.

Right. The location of a piece of land determines whether it is suitable for growing crops. In Tsegi Canyon there is fertile soil and enough precipitation to produce corn and pumpkins.

On p. 110. Goat kids are a valuable possession for Navajo families.

CRAFTS

Weaving

According to legend, "Spider Woman" taught the Navajo how to weave. Scholars see weaving as another early borrowing from the Pueblos. This theory is supported by clear parallels in the choice of patterns back to the earliest surviving pieces, and also in the construction and mechanisms of the looms (e.g., the heddle loom, the vertical loom frame). But whereas in the Pueblo tradition it was the men who did the weaving, among the Navajo the women took over this task from the very beginning. Moreover, Navajo women in time departed from the designs of their Pueblo models, creating new styles, especially under the influence of weavers from Saltillo, Mexico.

Using functional and stylistic criteria, experts distinguish a number of phases and subphases in the development of the Navajo art of weaving. From 1650 until 1868, the "Classic Period," the Navajos wove blankets, shirts, dresses, and shawls principally for their own use; they then traded their surplus production to other Native American groups. The finely crafted "chief's blankets" were very popular male garments far beyond Navajo territory, to the Central Plains and the Great Basin. In pattern and weave the chief's blankets resembled the similarly prized serape, the form of poncho derived from the clothing of Spanish shepherds. Production of these goods ceased when the Navajo in Bosque Redondo began to wear American-style clothing and mackinaw Indian blankets from the Hudson's Bay Company provided to them by the army administrators.

The "Transitional Period" (1868–1890) is characterized by a departure from the long-established ways of weaving and from traditional patterns (especially stripes and diamond shapes). Imported yarns and aniline dyes came into play. The weavers experimented with new patterns, the so-called "eye dazzlers": dizzying interlocking figures and ornamental designs in contrasting colors. These designs were a response to pressures from traders seeking to please far-off customers. During the "Rug Period" (1890–1920) the influence of the traders was even more decisive: Instead of thin, tightly woven blankets, the Navajos produced thick, heavy rugs (often from cotton yarns) suitable for the floors of Victorian homes. Even the designs of the rugs—with their oriental patterns and ornamental borders—show the influence of traders. Through the railroad, which now reached Navajo territory, the rug trade bloomed almost overnight. Catalogs were published, showing patterns, prices, photographs of the women who had woven the rugs, and anecdotal accounts of the origin of each design.

Of all the various weaving techniques developed throughout this time, plain weave is of particular interest, because it was (and is) most widely used. Each weft strand is brought over one warp thread, then under the next, and so forth. The higher quality of older specimens is visible from their denser weave and from the natural colors produced with vegetable or mineral dyes. (One exception is bayeta red, threads of which were unraveled from commercially woven bolts of cloth.) Most of the rugs marketed in the last 50 years have been treated with chemical dyes, which produce the more intense color effects that tourists generally prize.

With the reorientation of weaving from 1890 onward, various regional styles developed, named for individual trading posts. According to Ruth Roessel, an expert in Navajo crafts, the rugs from Chinle, Wide Ruins, and Klagetoh (Arizona) are of the highest quality; they are colored exclusively with vegetable dyes. The Two Gray Hills and Crystal, New Mexico rugs were woven from either undyed or vegetable-dyed wool. Teec Nos Pos rugs resemble those from around Two Gray Hills but were made with a combination of vegetable and aniline dyes. Lukachukai, Arizona is the center for "Yeibechai" rugs, woven with *Yei* figures representing benevolent Holy People. Ganado, Arizona offered rugs with an intense red coloration. Coal Mine Mesa, Arizona was able finally to restore the high standards of earlier times and is now the only source for large pieces, six feet by nine feet.

It takes some 215 hours to weave a rug three feet by five feet; the entire process, including shearing the sheep, spinning, dyeing, and selling the finished product, comes to 345 hours. A rug of this size sold to a trader in 1973 for $105, making the hourly wage approximately 30 cents. This example, calculated for the locality Many Farms, Arizona in 1973 by the Navajo Studies Department of Navajo Community College, makes it clear that the women who actually produced such rugs were very poorly compensated for their labors. Since that time the sale price has been brought more in line with the actual time required to produce textiles. Thus, weaving, the one measurable source of income for many Navajo families, has become more important, and the already prominent position of women in Navajo society further elevated. In 1972, traders bought $2,799,232 worth of rugs. Approximately 28,000 Navajo women played a role in their production.

Weaving is today a subject of instruction in Navajo schools. It can thus be assumed that it will continue to play an important role (especially given the continued high rate of unemployment) and that Navajo products, with their restored quality, will prevail over less-expensive Mexican imports. Navajos also enjoy the freedom of artistic expression afforded them in their work as weavers. They take pride in this widely recognized tradition, and they see it as a way of maintaining Navajo identity.

Silver Jewelry

Beginning in the Spanish colonial period (toward the end of the 18th century), the Navajo wore silver jewelry obtained through barter. They themselves manufactured jewelry out of precious metals, but not until after their return from Bosque Redondo. The first silversmith known by name was Herrero (*'Atsidi Sâni*), who learned his craft from Mexicans. The first artistically formed objects were made by melting down silver coins; the jewelry was not yet inlaid with gemstones as it is today. The ornaments were at first punched or engraved with awls or nails. Not until 1880 were the popular turquoises inlaid in the silver. The commercialization of jewelry making began in 1899 with the establishment of the Fred Harvey Company. Since the 1920s Navajo silver jewelry has been a "brand name" enjoying worldwide recognition.

John Adair, an expert on the subject, estimated in 1940 that some 600 Navajos were engaged in the manufacture of silver jewelry; by 1973 the number had increased to more than 1,300. In 1972, sales of silver jewelry to traders totaled $2,719,724. Moreover, silversmiths, like weavers, enjoy rewards that extend beyond the marketplace: They take pride in their craft as an expression of their rich cultural heritage. Valuable jewelry is also an indication of prosperity, and its beauty symbolizes the harmony so prized by the Navajo. Thus, although many hundreds of thousands of dollars' worth of silver articles were purchased by outsiders, and comparable quantities are in museums, the

▲▼▲

most beautiful pieces remain in the possession of Navajos living on the reservation where they were produced.

The tools of the silversmith's trade were at first quite modest: a small pair of goatskin bellows, an iron anvil (often homemade from scrap metal), an earthenware crucible, hammers, files and improvised engraving tools. Among the oldest forms of silver jewelry were the so-called *conchas* (Spanish for "shells")—round or oval disks that could be fastened to a leather belt. Belt buckles bearing simple engravings, bow guards (*ketohs*), finger rings, bracelets, earrings, bridles, necklaces (including those with the misleading name "squash blossom"), pins and containers for tobacco (often shaped like bottles)—all were made by the earliest Navajo silversmiths. Many of these articles are still made today, along with brooches, watchbands, money clips, tie clasps, cuff links and many more. Ornamentation and style have been refined considerably over the years. Gemstones, especially turquoises, adorn almost all articles.

Since the 1970s the silversmith's tools have changed completely. Modern soldering tools, diamond saws, electric polishers, metal saws and a wide variety of tongs now make the work easier. Raw materials, including either silver sheets or wire, are purchased wholesale from traders or in nearby cities. Turquoises and other gemstones (garnets, malachite, jet and now imported coral) come precut and polished.

Unlike weaving, the craft of the silversmith is rarely handed down in a family from parents to children. For this reason the Navajo Community College has offered training in jewelry making since 1969. Similar courses, for both beginners and advanced silversmiths, are offered throughout the reservation.

The demand for authentic Navajo silver jewelry has never been greater than it is today. The Arts and Crafts Guild in Window Rock, established in 1941 and supported by the Navajo Nation, strives to maintain the highest standards of production. Their concern is understandable, given the occasional unfortunate influence that the taste of outside buyers has had on Navajo style in the past. Many tourists want to bring back souvenirs, and they usually look for bargains. Thus, factories have come into being, off the reservation, to mass-produce copies of genuine Navajo artifacts.

Market experts claim that there are two basic categories of silver jewelry in circulation: heavy articles (bracelets with turquoise inlays, *ketohs*, rings, *concha* belts and necklaces) and the lighter ones especially manufactured for tourists. That such an easy or accurate separation between high-quality items for Navajo use and low-quality items for tourists can be made is doubtful. Such variations, if they do indeed exist, could be explained by the fact that many Navajos still own family heirlooms, more distinctive in style and more carefully made, and containing a higher proportion of pure silver.

Pottery and Basketry

Since their arrival in the Southwest, the Navajo have made simple, undecorated pottery, primarily for everyday use. Although their myths tell a different story, there seems to be little doubt that the Navajo learned to make pottery from the Pueblos.

Navajo pottery and basketry, however, have never been spectacular in design. Although decorated wares were occasionally produced in earlier times, the unadorned pot with a conical, partially flattened bottom later became standard. Until 1868, utilitarian earthenware vessels and traditionally woven baskets were found in every Navajo household. Pots coated with pinyon pitch were used for cooking or storing liquids. For certain ceremonies, food had to be prepared in a homemade vessel. Similarly, earthenware drums, partly filled with water and covered with hide, also had to be homemade for ritual use—for example for the "Enemy Way" ceremony. Another product of Navajo ceramic arts is the elbow-shaped or cylindrical tobacco pipe, often adorned with shell or turquoise inlays, and still smoked on ceremonial occasions as recently as the 1980s.

Beginning in 1868 the Navajo received metal pots, pans and ladles as annuity goods from the U.S. Army. Since the reparations soon included buckets, cups, plates and other household utensils, the Navajo virtually abandoned the production of baskets and pottery. After the government stopped the deliveries in 1879, the Navajo obtained essential household items from traders.

In recent decades, pottery making has been revived as part of a general renaissance of traditional Navajo culture, especially in the northwestern part of the reservation, around the Shonto trading post. The women who specialize in this craft have developed new forms and corresponding ornamentation for their products. Ceramics is now taught at Navajo Community College in Tsaile and at Rough Rock Demonstration School.

Clay is found in many places on the reservation, and potters can mix in pulverized shards of broken vessels. The Navajo method is to coil successive rolls of clay to form the body of the vessel; the potter then smoothes the surface with her hands. The pot is then coated inside and out with pine resin, as were the baskets of the 19th century. The firing takes place out-of-doors, in a "covered fire": The potter chooses an appropriate site, then covers the pot with fuel, usually sheep or cow dung.

Unlike pottery, basket weaving has not undergone any noteworthy revival in recent years; even the efforts of the Arts and Crafts Guild have had little effect in this area. Basket weaving, which like rug weaving is done mostly by women, is practiced only at a few scattered sites. Today the Navajo use baskets almost exclusively in religious ceremonies, and they generally acquire them through trading with the neighboring Hopis or Papagos.

On p. 117. Grace Ben, an outstanding weaver from Lukachukai, and her shepherd, Gilbert Harvey, shearing a sheep. Shearing is done in May and June. The wool is either used by the sheep owner (for rug making) or sold.

Below left. After it is washed, the wool is cleaned and combed.

Below right. The loose fibers are rolled by hand and then spun.

Right. Besse Greyeyes at her loom. As in Pueblo tradition, the Navajo loom is always vertical.

Basket weaving, like rug weaving, is done primarily by women. Sumac bark and branches and chemical dyes are used. Basketry, once an active art among the Navajo, is now practiced in only a few localities. Mary Black (right) and her daughters are famous for their work. Sally (center) has already won many prizes for her large *yei*-figure baskets.

Below. Balls of wool yarn ready for weaving, and parts of various plants used for dyeing wool.

Right. A valuable rug made by the famous Navajo weaver Barbara Teller Ornelas in 1990. Her patterns are influenced by Two Grey Hills designs. Barbara can produce a small rug of this size (15 x 39 in.) in two to three months. This rug has 90 wefts per inch.

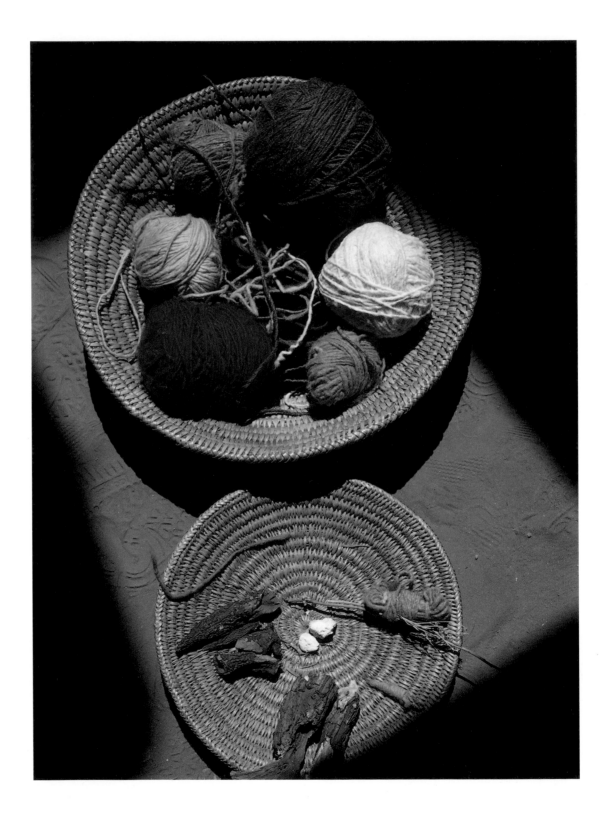

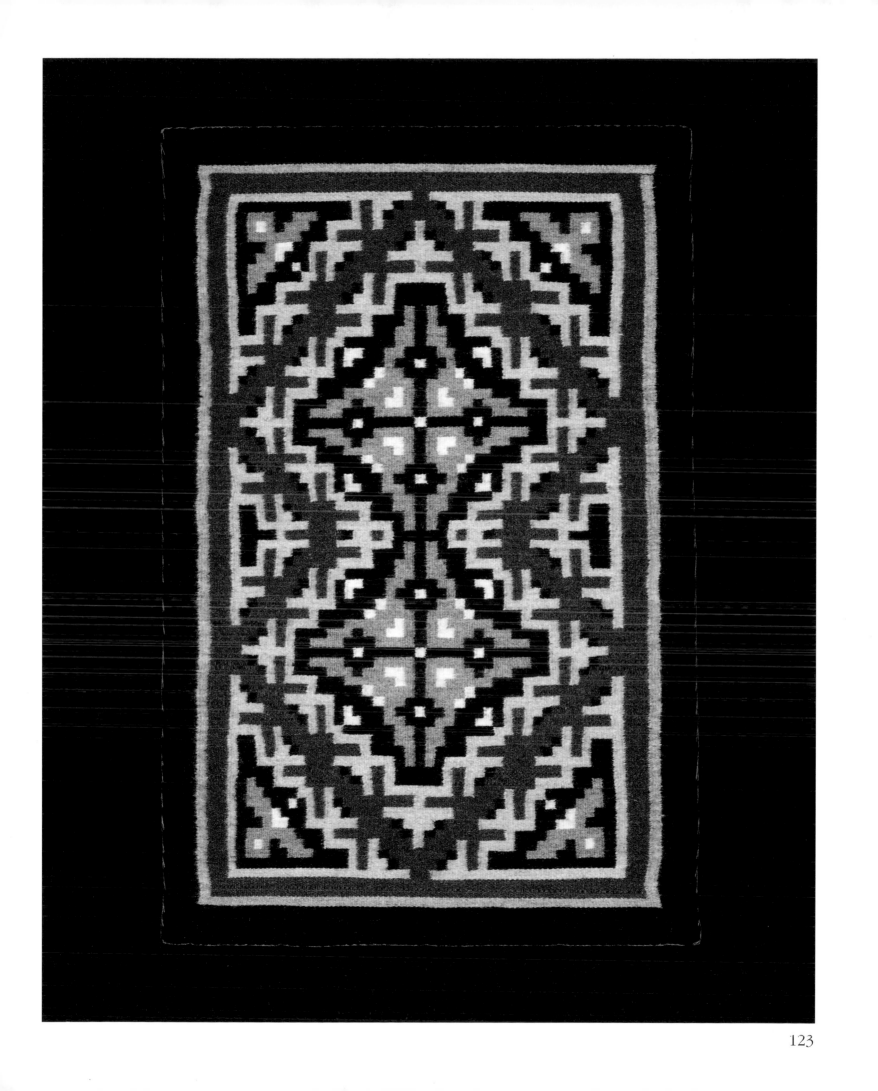

Below. Blanket (6 x 9 ft.) made between 1850 and 1865.

Top right. Chief's blanket (39 x 59 in.) made around 1900. For white and gray tones undyed wool was used; the rest of the blanket was colored with aniline dyes.

Bottom right. Pictorial blanket (59 x 79 in.) also made around 1900. All three blankets, Arizona State Museum, Tucson.

On pp. 126–27. Young Telferd Greyeyes in front of his grandmother's loom frame.

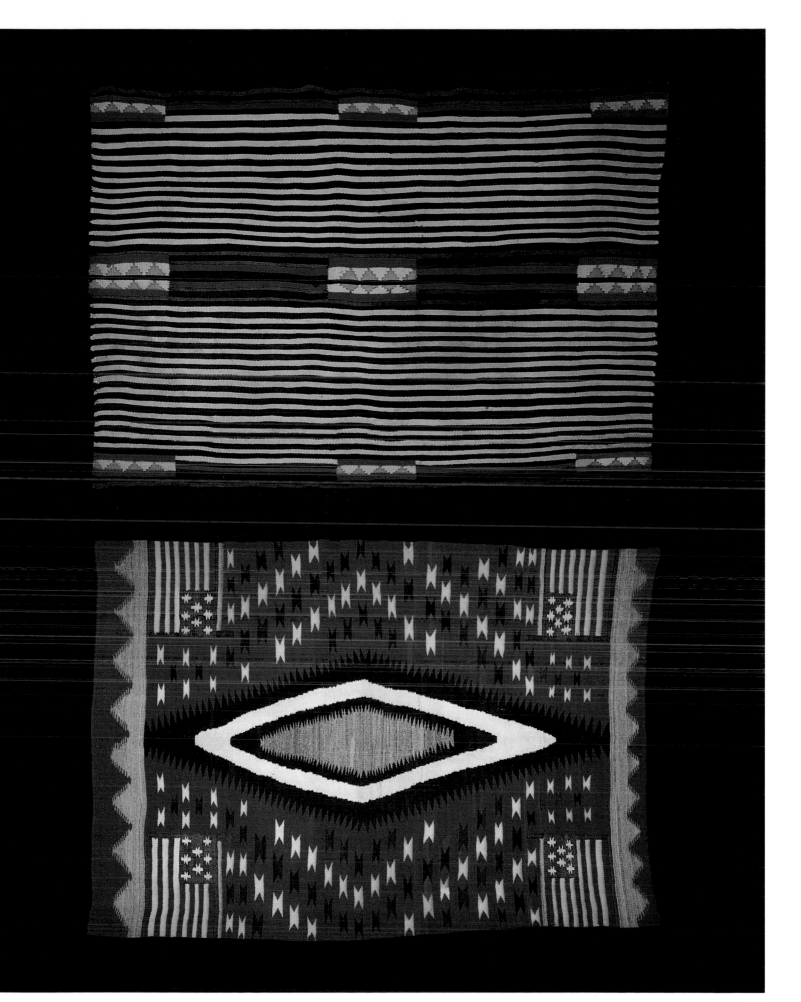

Below. Navajo silver jewelry is world famous. The turquoise is bought from a dealer.

Near bottom right. The artist Raymond Yazzie, from Ganado.

Top left. Raymond Yazzie's materials and finished products.

Top center. The well-known silversmith James Little, who also works with gold and precious stones.

Top right. Creations by James Little.

Far right. Alvin Thompson uses sandstone molds to make silver jewelry. The technique is called "sandcasting."

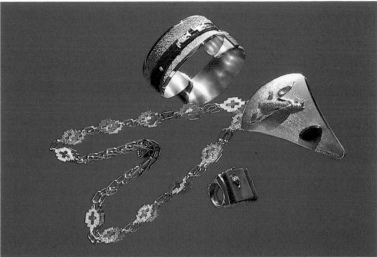

During the 20th century Navajo silver-smiths developed their skill with turquoise jewelry into an art form. A turquoise-nugget necklace with *jacla* pendant; five turquoise bracelets; one old and two modern rings.

Right. A so-called squash-blossom necklace with *naja* pendant; three turquoise-studded silver bracelets; a belt buckle decorated with coral; a ring; a stamped button; and a *bola* (tie). All items on pp. 130–131 from Arizona State Museum, Tucson.

Below. A clay pot with two *yei* figures in relief; made in 1990 by the potter Faye Tso in Tuba City.

Top left. Shards from prehistoric Anasazi pots are further broken with a millstone to serve as temper, then mixed into fresh clay.

Top center. All Navajo pottery is made without a potter's wheel. Rolls of clay are spiraled up to form the pot, then smoothed by hand.

Top right. The pottery is fired over an open flame or in a simple kiln, then coated with pine resin while the pot is still hot, to make it watertight.

Right. A young potter sells her wares alongside the highway to Shonto.

133

Above. Many Navajo artists are represented in the well-known galleries of the Southwest, especially in Scottsdale and Santa Fe. The sculptor Alvin Marshall uses alabaster and marble to portray typically Navajo and Native American subjects.

Right. The painter Baje Whitethorne combines Navajo landscapes with spiritual renderings of *yei* figures. He uses watercolors and acrylics.

On p. 136. Every Navajo woman is proud to wear her jewelry. Priscilla Neboyia has spent her entire life in the vicinity of Canyon de Chelly National Monument Park, through which she and her family guide tourists.

SOCIOPOLITICAL ORGANIZATION

Social Structure

Social relationships within Navajo society constitute a complex network combining family relationships and working-group solidarity. This system, which evolved over the course of countless generations, still constitutes the frame of reference many Navajos use to better understand the world and their place in it. Only the population explosion and the economic changes of recent years have produced upheavals capable of disturbing the traditional order to any noticeable extent.

The basic building block of Navajo society is the *local*, or *residence, group.* From an economic point of view, the residence group is the most important productive unit. Each of these groups has at its center a woman, the "head mother." Her household includes, in addition to her husband, all her unmarried children, her married daughters and their husbands, and all the grandchildren from these marriages. All female members of a residence group are descended from the head mother; adult males join this matrilineage by marrying into the family.

If a newly married couple want a household of their own, they will generally choose a location near the wife's family. A Navajo male, in other words, typically lives "uxorimatrilocally"—that is, in the same community as his mother-in-law. An exception can be made, however, if the land of the preferred living group (his mother-in-law's group) is not adequate to feed the children that the newlyweds hope to have one day, or if the bridegroom's living group needs the help of the young couple. Even if both mothers are still alive, the couple is not obligated to settle down with or near the bride's mother: They can choose to join either one of the two family groups, or to set up a totally independent household. However, once the marriage has withstood the test of time, the husband will find himself drawn more and more into his mother-in-law's local group, until he is fully integrated. This bond can now be broken only by divorce, separation or death. If husband and wife separate or if the wife dies, the husband goes back to his parents' residence,

▲▼▲

unless he marries another woman from the household—a sister-in-law, for example. In any case, any children from the first marriage stay in their maternal grandmother's household.

When the matriarch dies, the community soon dissolves; at this point, each of the individual families has traditionally set up a separate household of its own. In this era of overpopulation and land shortages, however, this arrangement is usually impossible. Today, more and more often, a Navajo couple chooses a home site on the basis of economic considerations, often settling near their workplace, ignoring the dictates of tradition.

The traditional focal point of a residence group is the communal herd, into which all the members—whether by birth or by marriage (but in the latter case often not until years after the wedding)—introduce their sheep. The community also has a piece of land, whose harvest benefits all the members. The group thus functions as an economic organism, committing individuals to perform tasks in cooperation with the rest of the community. In a special way, the identity, well-being, and status of a residence group were—and, to some extent, still are—determined by the condition and size of the communal herd of sheep. At the age of five, children were given lambs to help them develop a rapport with animals, and they learned to assume responsibility for the care of both their personal lambs and the herd of the entire group. The prestige of a Navajo was measured by the number of his or her sheep. Even a man who had married into the group could rise to become the leader or spokesperson for the group by virtue of his accomplishments as a shepherd. In time, however, many Navajos came to focus more and more on the priorities of the marketplace. Cattle raising became more important and sheep herding less so, which reduced the prominence of the traditional living unit as the basis and mainstay of the Navajos' social structure.

The residence group is, however, only one of the pillars of Navajo society. The second essential element is kinship structure and the rules relating to it. Residence groups are involved in issues of access to resources; the kinship system, on the other hand, determines an individual's social position on the basis of birth and membership in a social category. Relationships through marriage are also determined by the kinship system.

In the matrilocally organized society of the Navajos, the matrilineages mentioned above are the principal building blocks of the kinship system. An extension of these simple lines of descent is found in the matriclans, which

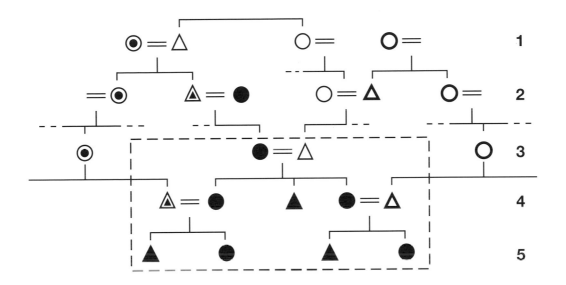

**Matrilocal Residence Group with Preferred
Marriage Partners for Women of the Fourth Generation**

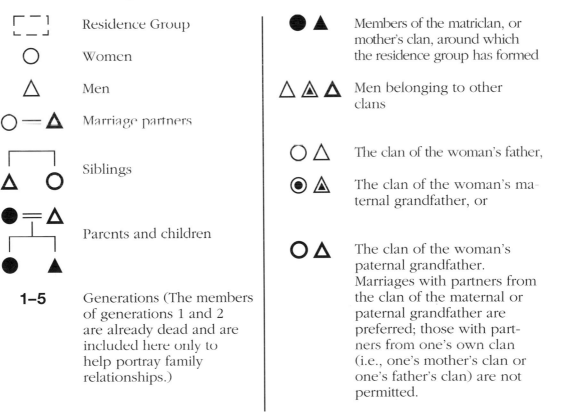

⌐ ¬
| Residence Group

○ Women

△ Men

○—△ Marriage partners

⌐—¬
△ ○ Siblings

●=△
|
● ▲ Parents and children

1–5 Generations (The members of generations 1 and 2 are already dead and are included here only to help portray family relationships.)

● ▲ Members of the matriclan, or mother's clan, around which the residence group has formed

△ ▲ △ Men belonging to other clans

○ △ The clan of the woman's father,

◉ ▲ The clan of the woman's maternal grandfather, or

○ △ The clan of the woman's paternal grandfather. Marriages with partners from the clan of the maternal or paternal grandfather are preferred; those with partners from one's own clan (i.e., one's mother's clan or one's father's clan) are not permitted.

▲▼▲

are not confined to local residence groups. The matriclan, sustained by distinctly marked group identification, is the basis for the active solidarity of its members, regardless of whether they live in the same place. The Navajos distinguish approximately 60 of these clans. They are linked regionally in groups of five or six, which were often originally a single clan which then subdivided. Marriages within one's own clan, or group of linked clans, are considered incestuous, as is a marriage with a member of one's father's clan. The ideal partner is thought to be a member of one's grandfather's clan. This principle of exogamy leads to a visible heterogeneity in the composition of a residence group, since the men who marry into it come from other clans. Children always "belong" to the clan of their mothers. If one asks a Navajo what social group he or she belongs to, the answer is "I was born *in* my mother's clan," but genealogically the Navajo is obligated to say he or she "was born *for* my father's clan." The Navajo language preserves many such distinctions. It contains very precise words for degrees of kinship, differentiating, for example, between matrilineal and patrilineal relationships. On the other hand, all female members of one's mother's clan are called "mother," and all male members of one's father's clan, "father." Such usage is said by ethnologists to be "classificatory."

Kinship structures and the interplay of social categories can lead to an unusual system of everyday etiquette. Navajo mothers-in-law and sons-in-law are expected to maintain a "polite" distance from one another, communicating only indirectly via third parties, and avoiding even an exchange of glances. Conversely, in certain other kinship pairings behavior may be sexually suggestive and highly disrespectful. Both this sort of "mock coupling" and the sort of social taboos just spoken of are explained as being necessary to hold in check the tensions and conflicts that would otherwise come to the surface, given the very nature of the restrictive social system of the Navajos. It should also be mentioned that, in this clan-exogamous, matrilineal society, a child's biological father plays no major role in its rearing. He is replaced by the mother's brother, who serves as a teacher and mentor to his nephews and nieces.

A key word in Navajo society translates roughly as "solidarity." Each individual, having a strong sense of his or her own place within the system of kinship sketched out in this chapter, refers to the other members of the clan as *shik'éi* ("my relative(s)"). They are all linked by the principle of *k'é*, which can be translated as "love, cooperation, kindness, peaceful relations"; it expresses intense, lasting, mutual (and material) solidarity with one's relatives. These values are the cement that holds the Navajo Nation and the Navajo community together. Another variant of this social partnership relies not upon family ties but upon reciprocal moral obligations in the barter relationship. The exchange of goods follows a strict principle of even-handed *quid pro quo*.

Residence, neighborhood, socioeconomic solidarity and kinship are independent variables of a prescribed, canonical ordering system—and sources of symbolic values, duties, and entitlements that inform and regularize life in Navajo society. This system may seem strange to outsiders, but its survival in the midst of the dominant society of the United States, with its very different set of values, demonstrates once more the ability of Native Americans to adapt to their social and economic environments. It is unclear, however, to what extent this system will survive as the Navajos become progressively more integrated into the mainstream economy.

Political Organization

Like many hunting-and-gathering peoples, the Navajo originally recognized no central authority. Each residence group was politically autonomous. Only on major ceremonial occasions, upon the resolution of internal disputes, or for purposes of defense did individual groups join together temporarily under a respected leader. The *naat'áanii* (local group leaders) enjoyed great social and economic prestige, but this did not make them rulers: They were empowered to speak for their respective communities in negotiations with other Navajo groups, other Native American nations, or whites, and could make treaties—but only after consultation with the other members of their residence groups. With time, the diminished importance of crop farming and the growth of cattle raising required that Navajos become more mobile and form coalitions linking several residence groups; thus the influence of the *naat'áanii* declined. As the new coalitions were formed, they generally came to be led by wealthy men.

At the internment camp at Bosque Redondo, the U.S. administration imposed a new organizational structure, consisting of 12 groups defined by geographical origin, and appointed a chief for each one. The principal chief was Barboncito. He was highly respected and had signed the treaty of 1868 in the name of all the Navajos. His advisors were the prominent Manuelito (Daháana Baadaní) and Ganado Mucho (Tótsohnii Hastiin), along with a panel made up of up to 30 *naat'áanii*: Narbona Segundo, Cabra Negra, Barbas Güeras and other respected men.

When the Navajo returned to their homeland, the government agents maintained this provisional administrative system for practical reasons. They relied on the authority of each chief (an authority that was restricted to his own locality) to deal with problem incidents—usually cattle theft—and internal disputes without military intervention. It was only the prestige of the leaders that made this administrative system work; after their death, it soon collapsed. The agents then settled local conflicts by establishing a paid police force.

When oil and natural gas were discovered on the reservation in 1921, U.S. administrators found it necessary to establish political responsibilities in a more formal, binding fashion. At first they tried getting all the *naat'áanii* in the petroleum-rich areas of the reservation to sign lease agreements, which provided that revenues would go in each case to the specific residence group on whose land oil or gas had been found. When the time came to contract for further drilling leases, however, it was agreed that revenues should benefit the entire tribe. This necessitated a tribal government, in which the residence groups in each of the newly established districts would be represented proportionally by delegates. In 1923 the Department of the Interior named a Commissioner of the Navajo Tribe, who convened a council of 12 delegates and 12 alternates. In the administrative structure of the time, the districts, each of which sent delegates, came under the following jurisdictions: San Juan (or Northern Navajo), Western Navajo, Southern Navajo, Pueblo Bonito (or Eastern Navajo), Leupp, and—later detached—Hopi (or Moqui). The organizational meeting of the "Tribal Council," as the representatives of all the Navajos were officially designated from this time onward, took place on July 7, 1923, in Toadlena, New Mexico. The most important topic on the agenda was the approval of various lease contracts for the exploitation of oil and gas deposits.

The Tribal Council, originally conceived as an advisory panel, soon proved more than ready to make decisions on its own. It brought about a

Navajo chief Barboncito.

National Anthropological Archives. Smithsonian Institution, Neg. No. 55,766.

Navajo chief Manuelito.

Photo by Charles M. Bell, 1874. National Anthropological Archives. Smithsonian Institution, Neg. No. 239.

Navajo delegates visit President Ulysses S. Grant.

Photo by Charles M. Bell, 1874. National Anthropological Archives. Smithsonian Institution, Neg. No. 2410-C.

change in the distribution of revenues from drilling leases, so that moneys were not distributed on a per capita basis to all the Navajos but went to the individual jurisdictions. Because of the threat of erosion through overgrazing, and also to keep Washington from reneging on the promised expansion of the reservation, the Council acted to reduce the total number of horses kept by the Navajo. Most importantly, however, the Council made all subsequent decisions as to the granting of prospecting rights.

The Tribal Council was reorganized in 1928. Women now voted alongside men—although their position in Navajo society had always given them a role in political and other decision making. The chairman and vice chairman were to serve for a term of four years. Legislative powers were still denied to the Council by the U.S. government, and a special commissioner had to be present at every meeting. Police and judiciary functions were not placed within the province of the Tribal Council until the 1950s. The creation in 1927 of the first "chapters" as community centers, originally intended to deal with grazing rights had the support of the Bureau of Indian Affairs. By 1933 there were nearly 100 chapters in operation; this form of organized self-help had proved to be a success. However, when the chapters became centers of resistance to stock reductions on the reservation, the Bureau of Indian Affairs refused further financial support for the chapters; by 1945 there were only 30 remaining.

The New Deal era brought a strengthening of efforts to promote Native American self-government. The federal government moved away from the course set by the Indian Allotment Act of 1887, which had accorded the property of the Navajo Nation to the individual families. John Collier, the industrious Commissioner of Indian Affairs, managed to persuade a majority of Congress that the rich variety of Native American cultures must be preserved. As a result, Washington supported efforts to preserve the territorial rights of Native Americans and to move toward more self-government; this was envisioned by the Indian Reorganization Act of 1934. But the Navajo and Collier soon disagreed over the mandatory herd reduction program. The Navajo viewed the program as an untenable incursion into rights already granted them—and as a serious threat to their survival. Collier was caught between two opposing camps: Congress and the Navajo Tribal Council. Petitions and letters of protest addressed to Washington, detailing the many inconsistencies of U.S. policy toward Native Americans, revealed the growing self-confidence of the Tribal Council and its leaders. In 1936 the Council obtained a constitution that for the most part followed the letter of the Indian Reorganization Act. But Washington was still reluctant to grant the Navajo sovereign control in the fundamental areas of economic planning, the courts and education. However, Washington did accept the Navajo proposal for the election of the Tribal Council: every four years 74 delegates would be elected by secret ballot, and the 74 would then nominate a chairman and a vice chairman.

When measures to combat erosion were stepped up in 1940 and a catalog was published listing draconian penalties for noncompliance, the Tribal Council voiced their agreement in principle but attempted, with some success, to grant special permits for small stock owners.

After World War II, Window Rock was declared the capital of the Navajo Nation. The executive committee of the Tribal Council was granted the right to assess punishments for violations of the law on the reservation—if the guilty party was a member of the Navajo Nation. Strong protests against continued restrictions on herd size finally led Washington to put the entire matter in the hands of the Council. The Navajo-Hopi Rehabilitation Act (1950) provided seed money for the development of the infrastructure and gave control of those funds to the Council. From this time onward, there were free elections of judges. The police force now reported to the central Navajo government at Window Rock. Little by little, the Tribal Council became an autonomous executive body. It also outlived the "termination" program of the 1950s, during which Congress tried to end the reservation system and the special legal status of Native Americans.

Capable Navajo leaders further stabilized the government of the reservation by reestablishing the chapters of the 1920s, '30s and '40s. By 1974 there were once again more than 100 of these small, effective bodies.

With increased responsibility came the need for internal changes. Various administrative departments were created, with strictly defined responsibilities; non-Indian specialists were hired to train Navajos as administrators. The Council itself now administered irrigation, emergency relief, welfare, the distribution of farm surplus and scholarship programs, as well as businesses owned by the Navajo Nation, including two motels. There were also occasional setbacks, resulting from factional conflicts and personal jealousies among local leaders. Thus, majority decisions relating to mineral rights (for example, a coal mining concession for the Black Mesa area, granted to the Peabody Coal Company) met with resistance.

After Washington had definitively turned away from the termination policy, it came to support the Council's plan to revive the traditional values of Navajo culture—partly through the introduction of bilingual education, which elevated the status of the Navajo language, and through the promotion of "contract schools." Now the Council even had jurisdiction over the appointment of BIA employees, and a Navajo Supreme Court was established.

The Council and the most important department heads—all Navajos—are now virtually independent of Washington. The Navajo Nation (as it has been officially called since 1969) claims cultural and political autonomy, not unlike that of each of the 50 states. In 1970 Peter MacDonald, an engineer by training, was elected chairman of the Council, after distinguishing himself as Director of the Office of Navajo Economic Opportunity. In the eyes of his many traditionalist detractors, MacDonald is a far too naive prophet of progress. In his three terms of office, however, he powerfully influenced the course of the Navajo Nation in the direction of increased autonomy. During his second term he brought about increased utilization of petroleum and mineral wealth—never losing sight of economic and ecological issues. As a result, he headed for a time the Council of Energy Resource Tribes (CERT), the "Indian OPEC."

In November, 1990, Peterson Zah was elected president of the Tribal Council, replacing the former chairman MacDonald. MacDonald had been barred from running for the newly created post of president because it was discovered he accepted bribes and misused public funds while in office. Despite these setbacks, the Tribal Council, made up of well-educated members focusing on economic growth, has won the respect of the state and federal governments. The Navajo maintain an office in Washington devoted to the interests of all Native Americans.

Top. Raymond and Colina Yazzie support themselves as silversmith and rug weaver, respectively. They live in a modern mobile home in Ganado.

Bottom. Tommy Roy, of Lukachukai, on an outing with his wife and children.

Right. In the remote parts of Monument Valley, some families still lead a traditional life. Note the hogan in the distance, left, and the arbor, or *ramada*, in the foreground.

On p. 149. This abandoned hogan on the Rainbow Plateau shows solid construction out of pinyon beams; the layer of mud originally used to seal the structure has washed away.

On pp. 150–51. A new settlement on the road to Crystal, New Mexico.

The family of Besse and Pete Greyeyes in their hogan. *Top.* Besse sits with her daughter Avyleni and grandson Telferd.

Bottom. Avyleni's older son Lee is raising a motherless kid in the warm hogan.

Right. Besse and Pete with their younger daughter Nadine and grandsons Telferd and Lee.

On pp. 154–55. A remote dwelling on Navajo Creek. Water barrels must be brought in by mule-drawn wagons.

Below. A Navajo family's home: an old stone hogan with a smokestack poking through its mud roof, next to a modern house with a television antenna and an automobile. In the background, the volcanic cone of Shiprock.

Right. Pete Greyeyes, following tradition, wears his long hair tied in the back.

Jackson Greymountain, 87, lives with his family near Navajo Mountain in Utah.

Right. Jackson Greymountain with his wife and three of their grandsons on the campground in Betatakin, Navajo National Monument Park, where they have spent the night on the way to Farmington.

Top. The feather attached to the rearview mirror, as in almost every Navajo automobile, is said to ward off evil spirits.

Bottom. Gale B. Davis in his pickup truck. For the Navajo, the horse has been replaced by the pickup.

Right. Besse, Pete, and Avyleni Greyeyes on the way into town. They wear traditional Navajo clothing and jewelry.

Nadine Greyeyes in her older sister's dress and jewelry.

Right. Young Telferd Greyeyes is still tied into his cradleboard. Toddlers, and especially infants, feel secure in the traditional carrier. It allows the mother to carry the child around easily, even on horseback.

Top. Window Rock, for which the Navajo capital is named.

Bottom. Government buildings are situated beneath the rock.

Right. In the large, octagonal meeting room (designed to suggest a hogan), the Tribal Council meets for at least one week, four times a year.

On p. 168. Delegates of the Navajo Nation are elected every four years. Left to right: Ambrose Shepherd, former delegate of the Ganado chapter and member of the Board of Supervisors; James Henderson, Jr., state senator from Arizona; Samuel C. Harrison, parent involvement specialist with the Head Start program, Nageezie chapter.

THE RELIGIOUS WORLD

Traditional World View and Ceremonial System

Preliterate cultures store their centuries of experience and socioreligious knowledge in the myths that they hand down from generation to generation. The primary function of this mythology is to establish and interpret the order and origins of the world. Thus a civilization's notions about the forces of the universe and how they can be mastered or held in check by means of magic or ritual are linked to a network of beliefs that includes every area of life.

For the Navajos, religion is not detached from other cultural phenomena; rather, it provides a permanent link to the mythic roots of the community. The religious doctrine of the Navajo is founded on the idea that the uncertainties of nature, as they imperil one's survival, are to be dealt with not only by physical efforts but also, and more importantly, through the assistance of divine powers, which is to be sought by the entire community. Ceremonies symbolically reenacting the Creation, or enlisting a collaboration of metaphysical elements for the benefit of the human race, are thus a fundamental part of the life of the Navajo.

This ceremonial system, which has been preserved over the centuries, is still reverently followed by most Navajos. Observers from the outside world frequently either completely miss or severely underestimate the intricate interconnectedness of ceremony and socioeconomic considerations. Clyde Kluckhohn and Dorothea Leighton, who are among the most knowledgeable analysts of traditional Navajo culture, speak of the connection as follows:

> From one point of view, all Navaho "rituals" are socioeconomic, that is, they are techniques for securing food, restoring health, and ensuring survival. Yet this statement is also one-sided. It would be equally true to say that much "economic" activity is motivated by the desire to obtain the wherewithal for giving costly ceremonials.

This formulation may seen exaggerated, but it essentially captures the interaction between religion and economics.

Religious functionaries, called *hataalii*, are responsible for this entire area of life. They spend years learning prescribed texts and the accompanying rituals. Every rite, every song, every ceremony helps the Navajo master the crises, uncertainties and dangers of the universe and the world in which they live. Moreover, the ceremonial system helps to define and preserve a collective social identity. Every violation of divine law—that is, every departure from the received code of behavior—is immediately visible in the form of a disruption in the overall harmony. The violation can be diagnosed by specialists and treated by the *hataalii*, usually with prayer, sacrifice or the creation of a sand painting.

The knowledge and correct application and execution of these ritual acts are thus a "cosmoplastic," or more generally world-saving, means to help keep danger in check and to restore harmony to the universe. One person or the entire community can be healed of a disease or freed from a quarrel—indeed, immunized against reinfection. The Holy People, powerful supernatural beings, attracted to the ceremonial by invocatory prayers and offerings, judge the formal correctness and completeness of the ceremony. If everything is to their liking, they are compelled by the "ethics of reciprocity" to restore the old order—the balance of powers between people.

Hózhó—Universal Harmony.   The principal goal of all ceremonies is the preservation or restoration of universal harmony. The individual can thrive only when the community is healthy and at peace with surrounding nature. Conversely, the well-being of the individual makes the entire community prosper. Thus, Navajos pursue the health and welfare of the individual, the security of each household, and the accumulation of ceremonial possessions, such as a white shell or turquoise bead to ward off lightning or snakebite. They also have less concretely targeted, but in no way insignificant, social ambitions, such as augmenting their prestige by arranging costly ceremonies and meetings. All of this is called *hózhó*, which is often (but inadequately) translated as "good, beautiful, blessed." The word encompasses the focal point of Navajo religious thought and activity, the fundamental framework of existential values. If the suffix *-jí* ("direction, side, manner, way") is added to *hózhó*, the word *hózhójí* is formed, the name for the most important ritual in the entire ceremonial system of the Navajo: the "Blessing Way."

Healing the Sick. Most Navajo ceremonies are intended to be therapeutic—either a response to acute illness or a proactive effort to prevent it. Navajos always combat illness through a combination of ritual and medicine. In this respect the Navajo approach is strikingly different from that of the Pueblos, whose ceremonies are most often fertility rites and rain dances conducted by organized priesthoods, religious societies, or other groups, as dictated by a set religious calendar. Among the Navajo, on the other hand, there are no religious societies and no organized priesthood; all ceremonies are performed, as needed, by specialists (called *hataalii*, "singers," because chanting is the most important component of every Navajo ritual) who are closer to the shamanistic tradition of the subarctic than to that of the Pueblo priesthood. The Pueblo ceremonial system is closely tied to the calendar and to the highly defined social organization of the entire community, whereas the Navajo system is more focused on the present needs of the individual, even though the entire group (usually close relatives of the sick person) participates in the healing process.

It is in the treatment of psychosomatic illness that these rituals are most successful, since they can function as suggestive psychotherapy, which can also reduce the organic symptoms. The prestige of the *hataalii*, his appearance, the mystical ambiance of the ritual, the communal experience shared with family and friends who participate in the healing process—all of this makes the sufferer feel better and recover faster. This therapy offers to all those who are present a confirmation of the fundamental axioms of their belief, providing consolation, care, and refuge as anchors in a rapidly changing world.

The Singers (*Hataalii*). Becoming a *hataalii* requires extensive training. Anyone who feels a calling to this office becomes the apprentice of an older *hataalii*, an expert with long years of experience with certain rituals; the novice pays the *hataalii* for this training. Usually *hataalii* specialize in only a few chants, because each chant is an extraordinarily complex canon made up of hundreds of songs and prayers. The apprentice must also learn the appropriate use of healing herbs and the art of sand painting. Women rarely become *hataalii.*

Many Navajos fear evil spells, which can be cast by *hataalii* who misuse their ritual knowledge by practicing witchcraft. The victims of such spells are not easily healed; they are treated by a sort of exorcism, which may involve the sucking out of an object that has been put into the body by the spell.

Spirits and Demons.   Every ceremony contains references to supernatural beings, the Holy People and other deities that sometimes take on human form: animals, plants, mountains, natural phenomena, and mythical creatures, like the ice giant of the North or sea monsters. These spirits each have their own individual characteristics, and every living creature is caught between their opposing forces. Many spirits can appear in multiple forms and play a variety of roles; in some cases this makes it difficult to distinguish among them. Evil exists alongside good in a complementary duality. Mortals must work to maintain harmonious relations with all the supernatural powers—an unstable equilibrium at best. The spirits sustain a person who lives in accordance with their commandments, but they punish infractions severely.

According to the Navajo myth of creation, the Holy People (*diyin dine'é*) originally lived beneath the surface of the earth. They moved from one subterranean world to the next, driven by magic forces. In the uppermost of the four underworlds they split into two factions, this discord producing the two sexes, and the female Holy People gave birth to monsters. A great flood washed all the Holy People to the surface of the earth, where they created the "first things." Then death overtook one of the Holy People. At the same time, Changing Woman (*'Asdzáá Nádleehé*) was born. When she reached puberty, the rays of the sun and the spray of a waterfall impregnated her, and she gave birth to two sons. These hero twins traveled to the house of their father, the sun, had many adventures, and slew all of the monsters except for hunger, poverty, old age and dirt. Changing Woman, her husband, and the twins form the Holy Family, which has a position of great prominence in the myths of the Navajo. Its members created the world and the earth surface people, the ancestors of the Navajo, and taught them what they needed to know in order to survive: how to feed and house themselves, marry, travel, trade, and protect themselves against disease, hunger and war. The Holy

People then vanished from the Earth, and the various Navajo clans began their migration to their present homeland.

The most popular of the Holy People is Changing Woman, the mother-creator of the Navajo. She is the most important figure in the myth of creation, and it is she in particular who taught the inhabitants of the Earth to control not only animals but also the forces of nature, wind, rain, lightning. The Blessing Way ceremony dramatizes her gift of her powers to humanity and her knowledge about (and control of) the things of this world.

The sun, her husband, clearly plays a less important role, but he did give mortals control over the elements. The hero twins, *Naayéé' Neizghání* ("Monster Slayer") and *Tó Bájíschíní* ("Born for Water"), are invoked at almost every ritual. Their adventures provide the ideals toward which every adolescent Navajo strives.

In addition to the creation myth (which contains numerous borrowings from Pueblo lore), there are offshoot legends of how individual ceremonies came to be—the misfortunes of a hero or heroine who through some misdeed ended up in a difficult situation and needed supernatural assistance. These serve as examples, codifying the proper performance of ritual. Many mythical motifs recur in the most varied of contexts. A storyteller generally begins with the myth of creation and then makes a transition from it to the myth that is appropriate for the situation at hand.

Stories dealing with other mythic figures pale by comparison with the tradition of the Holy Family. Some of these secondary figures, however, are almost as popular: the adventurous coyote, a rogue who is always making mischief and chasing women; or the *yé'ii*, who at the time of major healing rituals (Night Chant, Mountain Chant) are represented by masked dancers begging from door to door.

The spirits of the dead are an especially dangerous group of supernatural beings, not belonging to the Holy People. The Navajo do not share the Christian belief in the immortality of the soul. Their realm of the dead is full of dangers that are only vaguely perceptible. For this reason, Navajos dread death and all that is associated with it. They bury the dead quickly and try to forget them—but fear the return of their spirits to the world of the living. Only those who have died in old age, and the stillborn, pose no threat to the living. A ghost is thought to be the "evil part" of a dead person. It comes back to avenge any mistreatments that the person suffered during his or her lifetime.

The ghost appears after dark, in human form or as a coyote, duck, whirlwind, or some other creature or phenomenon. It makes specific sounds by which it can be recognized, and even physically assaults the living.

The Blessing Way Ceremony (Hózhǫ́ǫ́jí).   The Blessing Way (for which there are today five variants, depending on the purpose) is the most important and most frequently celebrated Navajo ceremony. Strictly speaking, it is group therapy, with no one specific therapeutic orientation. The Holy People, and especially Changing Woman, are asked to provide good fortune and happiness, long life, wealth, assistance with childbirth, or protection from harm. The Blessing Way is also used to install the leaders of local groups, to ask for a blessing on departing or returning soldiers, to strengthen *hataalii* novices during their apprenticeship, or to consecrate a marriage.

Kinaaldá, the puberty ceremony for girls and one of the most important social institutions of the Navajos, is also part of the Blessing Way. Even *Anaa'jí* ("Enemy Way"), an obsolete war ritual that has been modified to become a way of averting black magic, includes at least one Blessing Way chant near the end to correct any mistakes and/or omissions and ensure the effectiveness of the ceremony.

The Blessing Way ceremony usually begins after the hogan in which the meeting takes place has been sanctified with corn meal. Prayers are said, and the *hataalii* chants for one sick person representing the entire local group. The next day there is a ritual bath that is part of every ceremony, and the creation of a sand painting (*'iikááh*). On a smoothed stretch of ground, highly stylized representations of clouds, lightning bolts, mountains, rainbows, the Holy People in human form, and the four holy plants (corn, beans, squash and tobacco) are portrayed with cornmeal, charcoal and colored sands. Such a sand painting can be up to 15 feet in diameter. It is created in a single day and must be obliterated by sunset. The sick person is positioned on the sand painting so as to be in touch with the Holy People. Then additional chants are sung and prayers spoken. The ceremony also requires a bundle containing earth from the peaks of the holy mountains and some small pieces of stone. The bundles (*jish*) may also contain prayer sticks. Several pouches of pollen dust are also required. (No herbs are distributed, but corn pollen is eaten during the prayers.) The Blessing Way usually lasts for at least two nights—Navajos measuring time in nights, rather than days.

▲▼▲

Three masked men, as they portray *yé'ii* begging for gifts in the Navajo ritual "Night Chant."

Peyote Religion

Now officially known as the Native American Church, the Peyote Religion has a syncretic doctrine combining elements from the Native American tradition (especially where ritual is concerned) and monotheistic Christianity. Despite the Native American component (which actually came from Mexico), it was viewed by the Navajo as a foreign religion and at one time lumped together with Catholicism, Protestantism and Mormonism. This prejudice has disappeared in recent decades, however, largely because of the ease with which peyotism has been integrated into Navajo ceremonialism.

Whereas among the Plains tribes the Peyote Religion had spread quickly around 1890 (soon after the last flare-ups of the Native American struggle for freedom), it had no following among the Navajo, who at the time lived in a period of relative prosperity. Only after the imposed livestock reductions in the 1930s did adherents to the Peyote Religion begin to form circles—over harsh opposition from whites and traditionalist Navajos.

In 1951 it was estimated that some 12% of Navajos had joined, and by 1960 the figure was already one Navajo out of three. This sharp increase came about despite Tribal Council policy, which even included an anti-peyote ordinance. Not until 1963 did this opposition to peyote begin to erode; in 1966 the Native American Church of Navajoland was formed by Navajo peyotists in southern Arizona, independent of the Native American Church (many such groups sprung up in subsequent years); in 1967 the ordinance was revoked. Today, more than half of the Navajos living on the reservation are peyotists.

Briefly, the Native American Church can be described as a pan-Indian, semi-Christian, nativistic, redemptive religion or movement. It is thus different from all other denominations found in North America. It is further distinguished by the consumption of peyote during religious services. Peyote (*Lophophora williamsii*), a cactus (not found on the Navajo reservation, incidentally, but principally in Mexico and Texas), contains more than 30 alkaloids, including mescaline—mind-altering compounds capable of producing altered states of visual, auditory, tactile and synesthetic consciousness. The Peyote Religion is *pan-Indian* in the sense, first, that it has attained some popularity among almost all Native American peoples from Mexico north and, second, that it emphasizes the commonality of Native Americans vis-à-vis white Americans. It is *semi-Christian* in that a part of its symbolism comes from *Christianity*: prayers implore the assistance of God, Jesus, the Virgin Mary, and the angels. Numerous other images, however, are of Native American origin, including many supernatural creatures from a variety of native traditions. The Peyote Religion is *nativistic* because it is defined as being specifically for Native Americans in its ritual details. It also presents itself, however, as *redemptive* in that it seeks to transform the soul of the believer. It does not seek to overturn the prevailing social order, or call the faithful to rise up against white domination; this makes it acceptable in the eyes of other Americans. The Church's leaders proselytize; the Church itself permits variations in the general ritual canon; and within the framework of each people's culture it provides spiritual experiences, not only through visions but also through discussions of problems and solutions; it is thus also considered a religious *movement*.

▲▼▲

A peyote chief learns liturgy from experienced elders. In the event of disagreements about matters of detail, the central church provides advisors, who usually urge the disputants to hold fast to two cardinal principles: the common belief in the same God, and the use of peyote. Liturgical variations, however, are determined for the most part by the personality and training of the individual peyote chief.

The peyote cactus is the symbol of the religion and the medium for entering into a dialogue with God in his omnipotence. Moreover, the eating of peyote is recommended for both mental and physical ills. This association is reminiscent of the traditional Navajo approach to healing: ritual and medicine are essentially one. Peyote is viewed as God's healing gift to the Native American people. Peyote brings health and well-being, and also softens the blows of fate and facilitates the search for quality of life. Finally, peyote undoes the curses of witches.

The Navajos' peyote ceremonies closely resemble those of other peoples. With the exception of four songs that form the basic repertory, the service is entirely improvised, consisting of songs, prayers, and the words spoken between the individual parts of the ceremony. In this respect, peyote rites differ from the highly standardized Navajo tradition.

Four people officiate at the service: the peyote chief or roadman, the drummer, the cedarman and the fireman. In the center is Great Peyote, an especially large peyote cactus always used by the peyote chief. The service takes place in a Plains type canvas tent or hogan. The participants sit on blankets in a circle around a crescent-shaped altar made of damp sand, on which the Great Peyote is placed. A fire is lit between the horns of the altar. Firesticks, sagebrush twigs, fans of eagle feathers, and other objects are placed at strictly prescribed places.

The four parts of the ceremony—the opening, the midnight and morning water rituals, and the peyote breakfast—are punctuated by intermissions and accompanied by the smoking of hand-rolled cigarettes, prayers, drumming, singing, and the eating of peyote. The participants are purified with cedar incense, and "opened" and refreshed by drinking holy water; a flute made from the bones of an eagle summons supernatural powers. The service lasts from nightfall to sunrise. All the participants take turns drumming and smoking their cigarettes, the butts of which they carefully place at the two ends of the altar as sacrifices and then later burn in the fire. Participants often seem to be

Peyote ceremony, as painted by Beatien Yazz, ca. 1959.

in a trance; some have hallucinations. As the roadman sings his morning song, the participants partake of water, corn, seedless fruit, and boneless meat—all things that Native Americans knew before the coming of white people. This sacred meal affirms the community of the participants and their communion with the divine beings whose help and consolation they have seen in their visions.

The readiness with which the peyote ritual has been integrated into the traditional system of Navajo ceremonialism can be explained by the central importance of the healing of the sick and the fact that the use of peyote seems to enhance long-standing ritual. For peyotists, God and the Holy People are "all part of the same thing," as David F. Aberle writes in his detailed examination of the Peyote Religion.

Whites had long warned against the misuse of peyote, along with that of all other drugs, until it became evident that peyote was not addictive. The

Peyote Religion—in the eyes of outsiders—is a religion of the oppressed. It attracts the most adherents on reservations where Native Americans are utterly dependent on whites for their economic survival and live out their lives in degradation. For the Navajo this was the case after the sharp livestock reductions of the 1930s. The new religion, identified with communal striving for identity and solidarity, offered a pathway out of economic crisis and its related depression. Today, at a time of severe socioeconomic rejection and breakdown of traditional values, the Peyote Religion is a means of cultural dissidence. Its moral code helps combat alcoholism, lethargy, and the danger of suicide, and eases other symptoms of the decay of an underprivileged society.

Missionary Activity

Although missionaries were and are active on the reservation in relatively large numbers, they had only modest success until the middle of the 20th century. Only after 1950 did large numbers of Navajos join the various Christian denominations. Even in so doing, it should be noted, they did not completely break with the spiritual heritage of their ancestors.

It is difficult to assess the importance of missionaries among the Navajo. In the 19th and early 20th centuries their primary activities were in the areas of education and medical care; direct evangelization played a lesser role.

The increase in Native American clergy doubtless produced the corresponding increase in converts since the 1950s. Until then, missionaries were largely dependent upon interpreters, and the few baptized Navajos were not equipped for careers as clergy. With increased missionary activity on the part of Baptists, and with fundamentalist denominations (including Assembly of God, Seventh Day Adventist, Pentecostalist and Church of the Nazarene) not placing great emphasis on the formal training of clergy, the number of Navajo clergy increased. In 1977 there were 203, most of whom had attended Bible institutes but not seminaries. At the same time the number of Navajo Presbyterians (whose church had long been active on the reservation) and Episcopalians diminished. The Methodist Church, similarly, accounted for very little of the increase in church membership. The Roman Catholic Church attracted a number of converts between 1898 and 1935, but its influence waned considerably after 1950. Its presence had long been confined to the south-central part of the reservation, an area where the newer denominations were later established near Fort Defiance. A further center of missionary activity was established in the region near Fruitland, where the Mormons were particularly influential. They had discontinued most of their evangelization to the Navajo by the end of the 19th century and did not resume it until the 1940s. Their efforts intensified in the 1950s, and toward the end of the 1960s it was said that they had converted 20,000 Navajos, half of whom continued to be active Mormons. This, however, is only an estimate, and it may well be too high.

It should be stressed that Christian notions found only limited acceptance among the Navajos. There was no radical renewal, only a selective blending of Christianlike behavioral ethics with the traditional religion of the people. The Navajo prefer the old rituals.

On p. 181. Spider Rock (*Tsé'na'ashjé-ii*), a 426-foot-high sandstone pinnacle in Canyon de Chelly. According to legend, Spider Woman once spun her web over the rock.

On pp. 182–83. San Francisco Peaks, near Flagstaff, after a winter storm.

Top. At weekly markets, dealers sell herbs, minerals, and other objects that a Navajo healer (*hataalii*) needs for his ceremonies.

Bottom. Rattles made from wild squash are used in the Peyote Religion.

Right. Medicine man Elliott Long in front of his hogan.

Top. A Navajo healer (*hataalii*) chanting. His long chants summon the Holy People (*diyin dine'é*) to retore the harmony of all things, which is disturbed whenever an individual is ill.

Bottom. The *hataalii* and his patient at the end of the healing ceremony. He attaches small shells to her hair to ward off evil spirits.

Right. Earlier, the *hataalii* takes from his medicine bundle the objects that he needs for his ritual. In the foreground is a bowl in which herbs are soaking. The patient, who recently had an eye operation, waits patiently for the *hataalii* to complete his preparations.

Top. Bull-roarer (*tsin dj'ni*, literally "groaning stick"), made from poplar by Emmett Lee in 1960. In ceremonies it is swung to imitate the sound of the wind.

Bottom. Buckskin medicine bundle and other ritual objects.

Right. Two ceremonial rattles made of untanned leather, painted and adorned with rabbit fur. The handles are wrapped with buckskin to hold the horsehair in place. At the tips of the rattles, 12-in. eagle feathers are attached with cotton thread. Also pictured, two dried peyote buttons, $1^1/_2$ in. in diameter, which are eaten during the peyote ritual. All items on pp. 188–89 from the Arizona State Museum, Tucson.

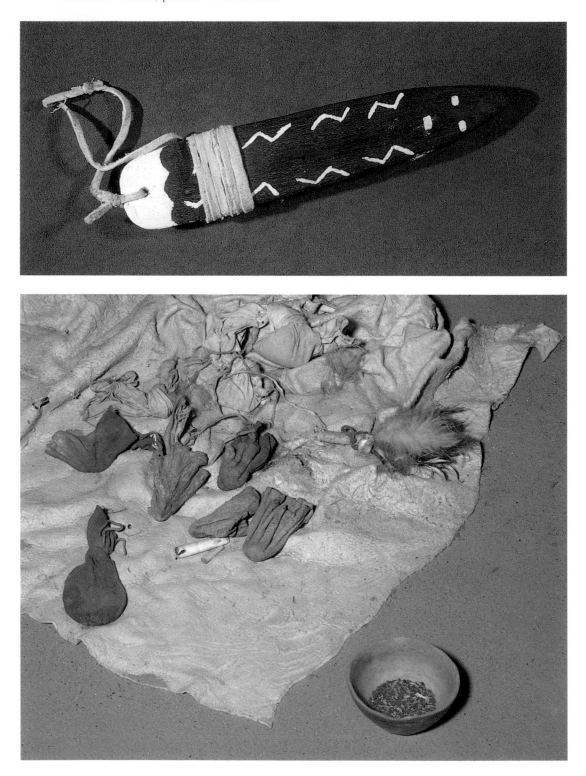

188

These 16 wooden figures by the Navajo carver Klitso Dedman represent *yei-bi-chei* dancers surrounding a patient (holding basket) and the medicine man (with bundle). Arizona State Museum, Tucson.

On p. 192. Watercolor reproduction of a sand painting of the Mountain Chant (by Clyde A. Colville, *c.* 1932). The two black figures represent the bear trackers; the white figures in the middle, the spirits of the mountain maidens. The rainbow's children are attached to the fanlike corners. Arizona State Museum, Tucson.

Top right. Watercolor reproduction (1980) by Laura Adams Armer of the firmament of heaven from "Male *Na'at'oyee* Chant." At the center, it shows the sky at sunrise (white), midday (blue), sunset (yellow) and night (black). The four horned figures represent sun (white), moon (blue), wind (yellow) and night (black). Between the figures are squash, tobacco and bean plants. The rainbow arches over the whole. Arizona State Museum, Tucson.

Bottom right. This reproduction by Laura Adams Armer shows the Crooked Snake People in the Beauty Way Ceremony, a peace chant. Arizona State Museum, Tucson.

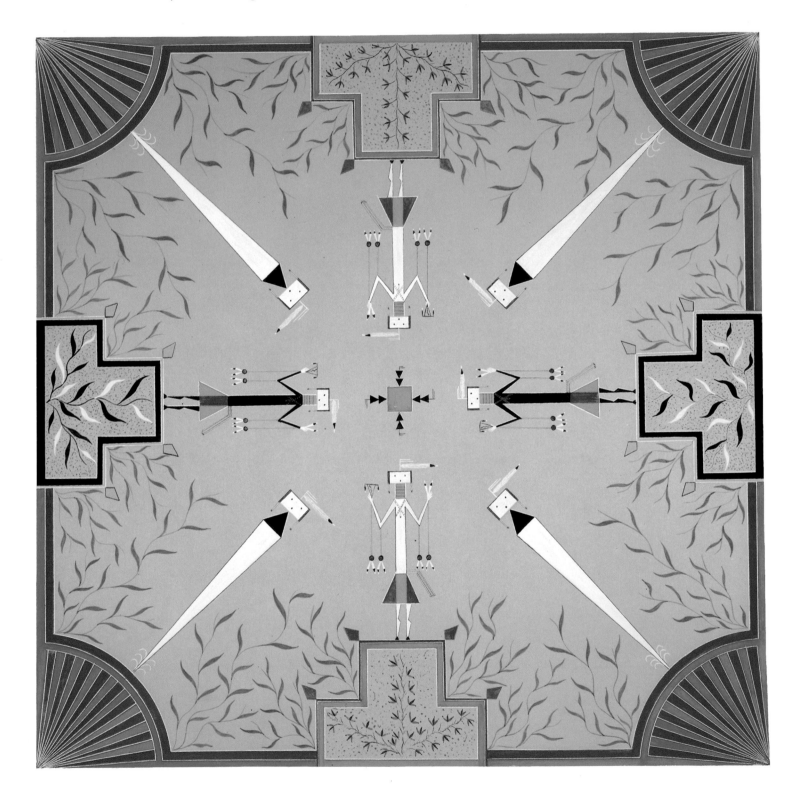

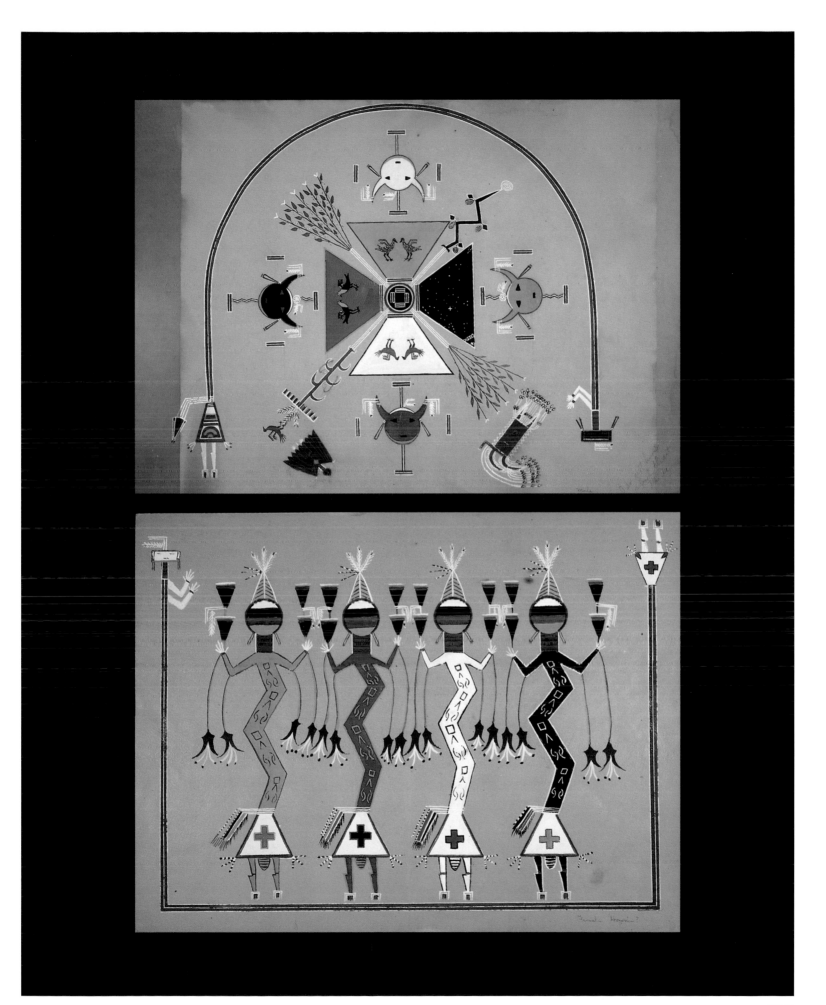

Below. This sand painting represents the house of the sun and is associated with the "Male *Na'at'oyee* Chant" from the Navajo story of the Creation. Displayed at Arizona State Museum, Tucson.

Right. The medicine man and chanter Herbert Ben demonstrates how a sand painting is made, at the Annual Intertribal Indian Ceremony in Gallup in 1990. This painting, of a corn plant betwen two *yei* figures, depicts the Harvest Day, a healing ceremony held in October.

The many small churches that dot the reservation indicate the variety of Christian denominations. Here, the Navajo Indigenous Church in Crystal and a modest cemetery.

THE MODERN NAVAJO WORLD

Formal Education

The treaty of 1868 called for the introduction of compulsory school attendance for Navajo children, but the efforts of government agents to enforce the policy after the opening of the first boarding school at Fort Defiance in 1883 had virtually no success. To the Navajo, Washington's attempt to force their children to attend schools run by whites was meddling, and they strongly objected on several grounds: They needed their children to tend their herds of sheep, which were particularly large at the time; they saw the taking of their children off to board at school as an act of estrangement, requiring the children to live far from home and thus removing them from the traditional process of socialization; and the school curriculum focused exclusively on non-Native American thought and culture.

Not until the 1930s, when John Collier became Commissioner of Indian Affairs, did an efficient school system begin to take concrete form, as part of the community development program. The project lost momentum during World War II, but, after the return of Native American veterans, the Navajos themselves became visibly more interested in educational programs.

The official goal of United States policy toward Native Americans was to assimilate them into American society. One means to that end was the establishment of public schools on the reservations. Therefore, in the 1950s such schools began to be built as alternatives to those already run by missionaries and the BIA. In the mid-1960s this government program received added funds under the Economic Opportunity Act. For the first time, some Native American teachers were hired, and a new curriculum was developed, tailored to Native American children. Additional BIA monies were available for parent participation programs, pilot projects in bilingual education, and teacher training; thus the Johnson-O'Malley Act of 1934, which up until this time had been the basis for funding of the Native American school budget, was no longer the sole source of funds.

▲▼▲

Mission Schools.　In Native American territories, the schools established by missionaries have the longest tradition. Considering their number, however, they have played a less important role than other types of schools. Still, they did graduate many leading figures in Navajo political and cultural life.

Among the most important of these schools are the Navajo Methodist School (established in 1912 in Farmington), the Ganado Presbyterian Mission School (established in 1906; closed in 1950 after the opening of the new public school), St. Michael's Catholic Indian School near Window Rock (the first, established in 1902), and the Rehoboth Christian Reformed Mission School near Gallup (1903). All of the older mission schools had outpatient clinics, as well.

BIA Schools.　Until the 1950s the Bureau of Indian Affairs was, with the exception of the mission schools, solely responsible for the education of Native Americans. At first the Bureau promoted boarding schools off the reservation (for example, the Intermountain School in Brigham City, northern Utah), and later on the reservation as well. Despite strong pressure from the BIA, attendance at boarding schools off the reservation fell off dramatically, leading to the establishment of day schools.

The parents had no say in the hiring of the (white) teachers or in the development of curriculum; thus, achievement levels expected by the BIA were not met. As a result, the bureaucrats wondered, in all seriousness, whether the Navajo children might be less intelligent than their white counterparts. A scientific study then demonstrated that school achievement is determined to a great extent by students' feelings of self-worth—that is, by their acceptance of their culture and language. The children had been asked, however, to rid themselves of everything Navajo and to become good little Americans. Nevertheless, even after years of schooling many children had an insufficient mastery of English; they got no positive feedback, their feelings of inferiority increased, and consequently their overall performance fell short of expectations.

The Navajo-Hopi Rehabilitation Act of 1950 called for the BIA to turn over to the public schools part of its responsibility—and funding—for the education of Navajo children. The federal government thus committed itself to financing public schooling for them. This enabled the BIA to fund the Navajo Education Emergency Program (NEEP), which included running trailer schools in remote areas of the reservation, establishing a number of new institutions modeled on public schools, expanding the system of boarding schools, and creating an educational program specifically tailored to the needs of the Navajos. For the first time, Saad (Navajo) was given the status of a language of instruction, at least for the early grades. In 1954 this ambitious plan, which took away the BIA's exclusive responsibility for Navajo education, was unanimously approved by the Tribal Council. Despite its assimilationist character, the new program was highly successful and reached thousands of Navajo children who would otherwise have had no formal education.

Public Schools.　Before 1950, Native American children, whose parents did not pay taxes, were not allowed to attend public schools, which were financed by state tax dollars. Only with the passing of Public Laws 81-874 and 81-815 were the schools opened to Native American children. Between 1952 and 1954, the BIA called upon the states of Arizona, New Mexico and Utah to take over the BIA schools at Mexican Springs, Church Rock, Sawmill and Window Rock. In addition, new schools were established at Window Rock, Ganado, Chinle, Kayenta, Shiprock, Tuba City and other locations. All children living within two miles of a paved road were to be provided with bus transportation to and from school. Improvements in the road system then greatly increased the numbers of students who benefited. At the end of 1961 over 1,000 students were attending public schools on the reservation. School transfers had reduced enrollments at BIA schools to about 15,000. Until the new system was fully implemented, there were constant disputes between the BIA, the states, and the Tribal Council about the use of funds and jurisdiction over the schools. In 1988, 41,394 students attended 160 public schools; 15,827 students attended 48 BIA schools.

Contract Schools.　Since the 1960s a steadily increasing number of Navajo teachers have come into schools that had formerly been staffed almost entirely by outsiders. The Navajo teachers developed a plan to seek methods for preserving Native American identity at the same time that students were helped to understand the Anglo-American world better. A new kind of school was established with funds from the Economic Opportunity Act in coöperation with the BIA and with the participation of the local community. Local

▲▼▲

committees, following the Navajo tradition of local group autonomy, were to oversee the schools.

The Rough Rock community was chosen as the site of the pilot project. The BIA provided a building and appropriated funds, and the Office of Economic Opportunity contributed an additional $329,000. Thus, in 1966, the Rough Rock Demonstration School—now known throughout the world—was born. The school board was made up of members of the Rough Rock community. It was empowered to sign contracts (hence the term "contract school") with teachers and have a voice in matters of curriculum. The Navajos considered the new school a victory for the Navajo people, and it became a center of community life.

For the 16 contract schools in existence as of 1988, Rough Rock continues to be a model. Now each contract school has its own curriculum, oriented to the particular situation and circumstances of the individual community (for example, its distance from predominantly English-speaking areas). Still, there are certain core principles shared by the curricula of all contract schools, just as they share certain problems (with the BIA, the Tribal Council and other authorities), going back to the terms of governance of the contract school system.

In accordance with the original conception of contract schools, Saad is the first language of instruction. In part this is because the majority of the younger students speak only or principally Saad. The children are given optimal opportunities for both cognitive and affective development. Only after they have mastered reading and writing in Saad is English used in the classroom and then introduced as a written language, as students gradually move into a curriculum corresponding to general United States norms. But Navajo studies remains part of the curriculum until graduation.

Generally speaking, comparisons show that students perform better at contract schools than at mission, BIA or public schools. Such demonstrated success is important for the survival of contract schools, because it guarantees the annual renewal of teacher contracts. Of course, this system of annual renewal makes long-term planning difficult. Only after assessing the financial situation can the school board decide what teachers can be renewed or hired. The majority of the teachers are now Navajos with teaching certificates (often earned concurrently with their first years of teaching), but the higher grades are still taught predominantly by outsiders.

▲▼▲

In addition to its pioneering work in the introduction of contract schools, Rough Rock, confronting a lack of usable teaching materials, has also become known for developing bilingual textbooks. The Navajo Community College Press in Tsaile, Arizona also publishes textbooks on Navajo history and culture. The government often supports such programs and recommends these publications to other schools for Native Americans.

The Role of the Navajo Government.   The department of the Tribal Council that has responsibility for the schools is the Navajo Division of Education (NDOE). It was established and continues to function with virtually no autonomy. It has, however, carried out a variety of advisory studies, and recommends students for college and university scholarships. Through these activities, along with its support of continuing teacher education (for example, at the newly founded Navajo Community College in Tsaile), the NDOE makes an important contribution to the betterment of Navajo education.

The Navajo–Hopi Land Dispute

Present-day conflicts between Navajos and Hopis in the so-called Joint Use Area go back to grotesque mistakes made by the federal government in the 19th century. A historical overview will help us to understand the present situation. The American journalist and anthropologist Jerry Kammer offers an excellent account of the political history of the conflict in his book *The Second Long Walk,* which provides the basis for the following discussion.

In 1882 the United States Congress laid the statutory groundwork for a reservation for the Hopi "and other Indians living in the vicinity." The land in question, almost 4,000 square miles (10,360 square kilometers), lay immediately to the west of the Navajo reservation of the time; the newly allotted land was a large, barren area far to the north of the principal Hopi (or Moqui) settlement. In time, the Navajo reservation was greatly enlarged with the growth of its population; finally, it completely surrounded the southern occupied part of the Hopi reservation, and conflicts broke out between the two ethnically different groups. The Navajo were then prosperous cattle raisers; the Hopi, farmers who had lived and worked on their land for centuries. The Hopi used the northern part of their reservation only occasionally, for sheep grazing, but felt that it, too, was a part of their heritage: This was the original homeland of their ancestors.

In 1891 the Hopi reservation was reduced de facto to 810 square miles (2,100 square kilometers), since the inhabitants had shown only passing interest in the northern "hinterland." Their principal activity was agriculture, and the northern land was ill suited to their style of intense cultivation. Moreover, the Hopi population had not grown so rapidly that they needed to colonize the vast north. The Hopi thus tacitly left the northern lands to the Navajo in their westward expansion; nevertheless, the treaty of 1882 remained in force. When the Navajo herd size was drastically reduced and grazing districts were set up for prescribed numbers of sheep, the Hopi were given District Number 6, which coincides with the present-day Hopi reservation.

When the Navajo granted a coal mining concession for the Black Mesa area in the northern part of lands formally allotted to the Hopi, the Hopi insisted on adherence to the terms of the old treaty. A federal commission determined in 1962 that 2,812 square miles (7,300 square kilometers) of the territory in question should be used jointly by Navajos and Hopis. Thus the Joint Use Area (JUA) was christened.

In 1971 and 1972 there were several clashes between Navajos and Hopis in the Joint Use Area, which received considerable news coverage, along with the activities of the American Indian Movement (AIM) at the time. Lawyers and politicians of every stripe attempted to resolve the problem. Hopi sympathizers, encouraged by Representative Sam Steiger of Arizona, pressed adherence to the terms of the treaty of 1882. The influential senator and Republican presidential candidate Barry Goldwater also took the side of the Hopi, after Peter MacDonald, the eloquent chairman of the Navajo Tribal Council, had refused to support him politically. Supporters of the Navajo included the anthropologist David Aberle, but Aberle's arguments attracted less media attention than those of a major politician like Goldwater. Representatives of the Hopi government called the conflict a "struggle for justice and [the] survival" of their people; Navajos spoke of a "victory of Hopi property rights over Navajo human rights" and called their projected removal from the JUA a "second long walk," likening it to the deportation of their people to Bosque Redondo in 1864.

The Hopi first obtained a ruling that in 1972 the herds of the Navajos living in the Joint Use Area (JUA) were to be drastically reduced (by approximately 90%) so that the Hopi half of the area would not be ruined by overgrazing. In addition, Navajo families were ordered not to erect, from that time onward, any new dwellings, schools, or other public buildings in the JUA. On December 22, 1974, Congress passed the Navajo-Hopi Land Settlement Act (Public Law 93-531), which provided for an equal division of the JUA within five years. In order that this partition might proceed as smoothly as possible, the government approved low-interest loans for the purchase of new houses and furniture. It also offered compensatory payments: A household would receive a bonus of $5,000 if it was relocated within one year of the effective date of the settlement act; $4,000, $3,000, or $2,000 if within two, three or four years.

Since Navajos and Hopis were unevenly distributed in the JUA, the district court for the area proposed that a dividing line be drawn, the Sinkin Line, defining the two sections. Navajo objections delayed the enforcement of the Land Settlement Act until April 18, 1979. Public Law 96-305 of July 8, 1980 clarified certain administrative details. On April 18, 1981, the joint Hopi-Navajo Relocation Commission proposed a new compromise draft which stipulated that additional land was to be provided for displaced Navajos; in addition, all elderly Navajos were to be permitted to live out their lives on their accustomed land.

After further delays, and concerted efforts by the attorneys on both sides to work out a mutually acceptable solution (efforts impeded by powerful leaders in each camp and by the support that each received from individual members of Congress), the federal government ordered that the Act be enforced on July 6, 1986, and that a barbed-wire fence be erected along the line of demarcation.

The resettlement involved some 7,000 Navajos (with other estimates as high as 10,000), widely scattered in the northwest part of the Joint Use Area, and over 100 Hopis. There was no discussion of the mining rights in the giant coal deposits located in the Big Mountain region, although the Hopi were doubtless interested in the fees that coal leases would bring them. The Hopi, moreover, showed no inclination to expand their modest herds of livestock, especially since the land that had been granted them did not appear well suited for grazing.

Eventually, in response to public pressure generated by an international media campaign, Washington decided to halt temporarily all resettlement measures. In late 1992 Navajo and Hopi leadership, in conjunction with the Interior and Agriculture departments, agreed to a settlement plan under which 400,000 acres of public and private land—distinct from the JUA, to the west of the present Navajo reservation—would be ceded to the Hopis, along with $15 million as compensation for the government's failure on behalf of the Hopi to uphold the 1974 Navajo removal order. In return the Hopi would grant 75-year leases to the remaining Navajo families living in the disputed territory, allowing them to stay. The plan required congressional approval to become law, and in early 1993 Congress was unwilling to back the plan due to opposition from white landowners in the area and outdoor enthusiasts. It seems doubtful that this 100-year-old land dispute will be resolved anytime soon.

Problems of Economic Adjustment: Mother Country and Internal Colony

From the time of the return from Bosque Redondo in 1868 until the 1930s, animal husbandry supported the majority of Navajos. This changed greatly, however, with the drastic forced reduction in herd size, as the precisely limited herds did not provide enough food to keep pace with the rapid growth in population. The Navajo were forced to seek other sources of income, and they found them in the mineral and petroleum deposits on the reservation. The exploitation of these resources, however, required that they integrate them into the U.S. economy, with its advanced technology.

David F. Aberle writes that this dependence on the larger economy has made the Navajo Nation a colony within the borders of its economic mother country, the United States. Mineral and petroleum deposits are exploited by U.S. firms that then undertake profitable processing and refining back at their own facilities, far from the reservation. The Navajo receive only leasing fees and—only recently, after complaints from the Navajo government—considerably increased royalties. The companies, on the other hand, make huge profits from the sale of the end-products.

The first large petroleum deposits were discovered and exploited in the northern part of the reservation in the early 1920s. The leasing fees were about $70,000 annually. From 1938 until 1956 the Navajos' income from oil and gas deposits increased to $1,000,000 annually. When new fields near Four Corners

▲▼▲

204

were discovered in the 1950s, the oil yield increased, and leasing fees and royalties climbed to more than $30,000,000. In the 1960s the yield fell off sharply; Navajo income, however, was kept level for a time through an increase in fees. In the 1970s and 1980s, the yield continued to drop, and income has declined accordingly, barely reaching $14,000,000 in 1987.

Oil and gas leasing fees and royalties benefited the entire Navajo Nation and helped considerably to stabilize the Tribal Council. United States corporations made contracts only with the Council, after early, unsuccessful attempts to reach agreements with smaller groups of Navajos.

In comparison with oil and gas revenues, uranium, vanadium and helium have been far less lucrative. Uranium leases brought in $2,100,000 in 1983, but that figure fell to zero four years later. As of this writing the last visible traces of uranium slag heaps are being removed from Shiprock, Mexican Hat, Tuba City and Monument Valley. The employment of Navajo laborers in uranium mines in the 1940s and 1950s had unforeseeable consequences: Through radioactive contamination of the ground around pits and slag heaps, many workers developed cancer. Only today is the full extent of the tragedy becoming clear.

As oil wells were depleted, the outside corporations turned to the exploitation of coal. Since it could be obtained through the inexpensive process of strip mining, costs remained low and the companies' profits climbed. In 1987 coal licenses brought the Navajos $28,000,000, or two thirds of their total natural-resource revenues.

With the explorations of U.S. mining concerns, especially the Peabody Coal Company, the Tribal Council succeeded in having some of its most important demands met, including the hiring of Navajo laborers, the sharing of information as to the value of mineral and petroleum deposits, long-range planning of mining activities, and—last but not least—higher leasing fees.

In the 1970s, exploitation of the huge coal deposits (approximately 600 million tons) at Black Mesa began. Coal obtained here—12 million tons annually from Black Mesa Mine and Kayenta Mine—is used almost exclusively to produce electrical power. The Peabody Coal Company transports coal from the Black Mesa Mine on a conveyer belt to a specially constructed rail line 78 miles long. The coal is loaded onto cars and makes its way to the Navajo generating plant in Page, on the Colorado River. This is the electricity source for most of the reservation. Air pollution from the plant has caused great concern, and has led Navajos living in the vicinity to protest its continued operation.

The Kayenta Mine, which contains the richest strata in North America, produces 7,000,000 tons of coal per year. The coal is crushed, then carried by water pressure for three days through a 270-mile pipeline to the Mohave plant on the lower Colorado River. This extremely inexpensive process produces no flue gas, but the massive removal of groundwater has disastrous effects on vegetation. Strip mining itself leaves ugly scars on the landscape, which can be restored only through major reclamation and restoration programs. Steps are now being taken in this direction.

Renewable resources also yield profits. Lumbering licenses in the Chuska Mountains and on the Defiance Plateau bring in $1,500,000 annually to the Navajo Nation.

All attempts to date by the Navajo to take over the management of their resources, or to enter into joint projects as equal partners of U.S. firms, have failed. The first impediment is the lack of capital, but there is also a lack of trained Navajo professionals, specifically in the areas of technology and management. The federal government provides no underwriting of joint ventures; it finances only welfare and human services projects. The beneficiaries of the natural wealth of the Navajo include not only big business but also the states of Arizona and New Mexico, for whom these resources create massive revenues in the form of corporate income taxes.

The Navajo have no control over the exploitation of their natural resources. Profits go to outsiders, and income in the form of leasing fees and royalties is used for the budgets of the Navajo government and for welfare payments, not for the capitalization of new projects. The largest single source of income for the Navajo government has been taxes levied on the reservation; in 1987 tax revenues from all sources totaled just under $250,000,000. The annual per capita income in 1969 was $776 (compared with $3,700 for white Americans); in 1979 it had risen to $2,414 (compared with $7,787 for whites); in 1989 it was $3,735 ($15,687 for whites). The average Navajo family still provides for its basic needs directly through animal husbandry and farming. The dollar incomes cited here come mostly from wage labor on and off the reservation. The Navajo government is the largest employer on the reservation, with its business arms, the NAPI (Navajo Agricultural Products Industry), the NFPI (Navajo Forest Products Industry), and the NTUA (Navajo Tribal Utilities

Authority), which is responsible for water and electricity, garbage collection and traffic. The Bureau of Indian Affairs, the Office of Navajo Economic Opportunity, the public schools and the Public Health Service also employ Navajos. Wages earned off the reservation are becoming more and more important; they guarantee a family a better standard of living than if they were dependent on wages available on the reservation. Nevertheless, half the population still have incomes below the poverty level (according to the 1990 U.S. Census). In 1987 the unemployment rate was close to 30%.

Under the circumstances, it is understandable that Navajos find it not only socially desirable but also economically necessary to live with their extended families. Only in this way can the individual find support in times of crisis. In the family circle, household crafts (such as rug weaving and silversmithery) also flourish. These activities often become small businesses, even factories. In recent years the preparation and sale of crafts products for the souvenir trade—for sale both on the reservation and off—has grown tremendously in importance. Articles associated with other cultures (Hopi kachina dolls, for example) are also made by the Navajo in great quantities for sale by national chains.

The Navajo government now faces a dilemma. Income from the exploitation of natural resources is not expected to continue beyond the year 2005, or 2025 at the latest, and no replacement is in sight. The population (165,000 in 1988) is increasing dramatically, and new economic programs must be created in the very near future. The greatest hurdle is the colonial status of the Navajo, which makes it impossible for them to take charge of their own economic development. The primary responsibility for this lies with the Bureau of Indian Affairs in its inability to prevail against the Department of the Interior and Congress. For this reason the Navajo government seeks a measure of internal autonomy, a political objective that may offer some hope for the medium-to-long term.

Future goals include developing the infrastructure, improving job opportunities, promoting skilled labor, obtaining available capital for the exploitation of natural resources (including those in national parks) and the development of light industry. The federal government is called upon to provide start-up financing for these projects, which should not enrich private U.S. corporations as in the past, but rather contribute to the dismantling of fossilized colonial structures unworthy of one of the world's richest countries.

▲▼▲

Right. Sawmill of the Navajo Forest Products Industry (NFPI), the largest enterprise owned by the Navajo Nation.

Coal mining in the northern part of Black Mesa. The high-grade coal is obtained from two large strip mines. Ninety percent of the 900 employees are Navajos, including women.

Clockwise from upper left. Another enterprise owned by the Navajo Nation, the Navajo Agricultural Products Industry (NAPI), south of Farmington, also runs the largest irrigation project for the reservation.—Pumping plants supply miles of irrigation canals.—Grain silos, in which wheat is stored until it is sold.—The NAPI has more than 500 permanent employees, 95% of them Navajos. During the harvest an additional 1,000 employees are hired.—In the same region there are also gas and petroleum deposits; these, however, are exploited by U.S. corporations; the Navajos receive leasing fees and royalties.

On pp. 214–15. Wheat is harvested between mid-July and the end of August with ultramodern equipment. The irrigation apparatus remains in place to foster the growth of alfalfa on these fields as a second crop.

Clockwise from upper left. Alfalfa and potato harvest.—Modern, efficient machines economize the process.—The potatoes are sorted on the spot.—An additional business activity involves purchasing cattle from nearby ranches and fattening them up for ultimate resale; 10,000 head can be boarded at a time.

On pp. 218–19. Highway 160, one of the main traffic arteries in the western part of the reservation, cuts through the Moenkopi Plateau between Tuba City and Flagstaff.

On the weekend, many Navajos leave their remote homesites and drive to cities such as Gallup, Farmington or Flagstaff. Here they shop, barter, look for a new horse or sell the silver jewelry, blankets and other articles they have made.

On pp. 222–23. The Navajo are excellent horseback riders. For this reason there is great interest in the bronco riding contests held annually at the time of the Intertribal Indian Ceremony in Gallup.

Clockwise from upper left. Navajo Community College in Tsaile, situated at the foot of the beautiful Chuska Mountains.—Two photos of classroom work at Rough Rock Demonstration School, which was opened in 1966 and is still a model for many new schools. Classes are conducted in Navajo (Saad) as well as in English.—Students at Navajo Community College celebrate at their graduation.

Left. At a commencement ceremony at Navajo Community College, Tsaile, congratulations are in order.

Below. Recess at Rough Rock Demonstration School. A fourth-grade student after math class.

Top. At the supermarket meat counter.

Bottom. The week's laundry gets done as part of a day of shopping in town.

Right. Cinches, hats, cowboy boots and lassos are offered for sale at a modern trading post.

On p. 232. Tommy Arviso, Jr. is the editor-in-chief of the *Navajo Times*, which is published weekly in Window Rock. The front page of this edition includes coverage of an auction of Navajo rugs at the Navajo Inn in Window Rock, another business owned by the Navajo Nation.

230

BIBLIOGRAPHY

Out of the vast wealth of publications on the Navajo, this list offers only a selection. Starred titles (*) were of particular use in the preparation of this volume. The abbreviation "HNAI 10" stands for *Handbook of North American Indians*, Vol. 10: Southwest [II], Smithsonian Institution, Washington, 1983; the 20-volume *Handbook* is edited by William C. Sturtevant.

Aberle, David F. "The Peyote Religion Among the Navajo." *Viking Fund Publications in Anthropology* 42. New York, 1966.
———. *Peyote Religion Among the Navajo*. HNAI 10:558–569, 1983 (*).
———. *Navajo Economic Development*. HNAI 10: 641–658, 1983 (*).

Adair, John. *The Navajo and Pueblo Silversmiths*. Norman: University of Oklahoma Press, 1944.

Adams, William Y. "Shonto: A Study of the Role of the Trader in a Modern Navaho Community." *Bureau of American Ethnology Bulletin* 188. Washington, D.C., 1963.

Amsden, Charles A. *Navaho Weaving: Its Technic and History*. Santa Ana, Calif.: Fine Arts Press, 1934; Glorieta, N.M.: Rio Grande Press, 1971.

Annual Report to the Economic Development Committee of the Navajo Nation Council: The 1989 Activities of the Navajo Agricultural Products Industry. Farmington, 1990 (*).

Bailey, Garrick and Roberta G. *A History of the Navajos: The Reservation Years*. Santa Fe, N.M.: School of American Research Press, 1986 (*).

Bender, Norman J. "New Hope for the Indians." *The Grant Peace Policy and the Navajos in the 1870s*. Albuquerque: University of New Mexico, 1989.

Bergman, Robert L. *Navajo Health Services and Projects*. HNAI 10: 672–678, 1983 (*).

Blomberg, Nancy J. *Navajo Textiles: The William Randolph Hearst Collection*. Tucson: University of Arizona Press, 1988 (*).

Brugge, David M. *Navajo Prehistory and History to 1850*. HNAI 10: 489–501, 1983 (*).

Brugge, David M., and Charlotte J. Frisbie, eds. "Navajo Religion and Culture." *Papers in Anthropology* 17. Santa Fe: Museum of New Mexico Press, 1982.

Commission for Accelerating Navajo Development Opportunities, Technical Support Department. *Navajo Nation FAX 88*. Window Rock, Ariz.: The Navajo Tribe, 1988 (*).

Commission for Accelerating Navajo Development Opportunities. *The Navajo Nation Overall Economic Development Program: 1988 Annual Progress Report*. Window Rock, Ariz.: The Navajo Tribe, 1988 (*).

Commission for Accelerating Navajo Development Opportunities. *The Large Farm—Dáa'ák'eh Nitsaa*. Window Rock, Ariz.: The Navajo Nation, 1989 (*).

Downs, James F. "Animal Husbandry in Navajo Society and Culture." *University of California Publications in Anthropology* 1. Berkeley, 1964.

———. *The Navajo*. New York: Holt, Rinehart and Winston, 1972.

Dyk, Walter. *Son of Old Man Hat: A Navajo Autobiography* [1938]. Lincoln: University of Nebraska Press, 1967.

Dyk, Walter and Ruth, eds. *Left Handed: A Navajo Autobiography*. New York: Columbia University Press, 1980.

Emerson, Gloria J. *Navajo Education*. HNAI 10: 659–671, 1983 (*).

Frisbie, Charlotte J. *Kinaaldá: A Study of the Navaho Girls' Puberty Ceremony*. Middletown, Conn.: Wesleyan University Press, 1967.

———. *Navajo Medicine Bundles or Jish: Acquisition, Transmission, and Disposition in the Past and Present*. Albuquerque: University of New Mexico Press, 1987.

Gilbreath, Kent. *Red Capitalism: An Analysis of the Navajo Economy*. Norman: University of Oklahoma Press, 1973.

Gilpin, Laura. *The Enduring Navajo*. Austin: University of Texas Press, 1968.

Goodman, James M. *The Navajo Atlas: Environments, Resources, People and History of the Diné Bikeyah*. Norman: University of Oklahoma Press, 1982 (*).

Grant, Campbell. *Canyon de Chelly: Its People and Rock Art*. Tucson: University of Arizona Press, 1978.

Haile, Berard. "Origin Legend of the Navaho Enemy Way." *Yale University Publications in Anthropology* 17. 1938. Reprinted as *Origin Legend of the Navaho Enemy Way*. New York: AMS Press, 1983.

Hartman, Russell P., and Jan Musial. *Navajo Pottery: Traditions and Innovations*. Flagstaff, Ariz.: Northland Press, 1987.

Hill, W. W. "The Agricultural and Hunting Methods of the Navaho Indians." *Yale University Publications in Anthropology* 18. 1938. Reprinted as *The Agricultural and Hunting Methods of the Navaho Indians*. New York: AMS Press, 1983 (*).

Iverson, Peter. *The Navajos: A Critical Bibliography*. Bloomington: Indiana University Press, 1976.

———. *The Navajo Nation*. Westport, Conn.: Greenwood Press, 1981 (*).

———. *The Emerging Navajo Nation*. HNAI 10: 636–640, 1983 (*).

Jett, Stephen C., and Virginia E. Spencer. *Navajo Architecture: Forms, History, Distributions*. Tucson: University of Arizona Press, 1981.

Johnson, Broderick, ed. *Navajos and World War II*. Tsaile, Ariz.: Navajo Community College Press, 1977.

Kahlenburg, Mary H., and Anthony Berlant. *The Navajo Blanket*. Los Angeles: Praeger Publishers for Los Angeles County Museum of Art, 1972 (*).

Kammer, Jerry. *The Second Long Walk: The Navajo-Hopi Land Dispute*. Albuquerque: University of New Mexico Press, 1980 (*).

Kelly, Lawrence C. *The Navajo Indians and Federal Indian Policy, 1900–1935*. Tucson: University of Arizona Press, 1968.

Kluckhohn, Clyde. "Navajo Witchcraft." *Papers of the Peabody Museum of American Archaeology and Ethnology* 22. Harvard University, 1944; Boston: Beacon Press, 1962.

Kluckhohn, Clyde, and Dorothea Leighton. *The Navajo*. Cambridge, Mass.: Harvard University Press, 1946; Garden City, N.Y.: Natural History Library, 1962 (rev. ed.) (*).

Kluckhohn, Clyde, W. W. Hill, and Lucy W. Kluckhohn: *Navaho Material Culture*. Cambridge, Mass.: Belknap Press of Harvard University Press, 1971 (*).

Lawson, Michael L. "The Navajo Indian Irrigation Project: Muddied Past, Clouded Future." *The Indian Historian* 9 (1), 1976 (*).

Leighton, Dorothea C., and Clyde Kluckhohn. *Children of the People: The Navaho Individual and His Development*. Cambridge, Mass.: Harvard University Press, 1947.

Leighton, Alexander H., and Dorothea C. Leighton. "Gregorio, the Hand-Trembler: A Psychobiological Personality Study of a Navaho Indian." *Papers of the Peabody Museum of American Archaeology and Ethnology* 40 (1). Harvard University, 1949.

Levy, Jerrold E., et al. *Hand Trembling, Frenzy Witchcraft, and Moth Madness: A Study of Navajo Seizure Disorders*. Tucson: University of Arizona Press, 1987.

▲▼▲

Link, Martin A., ed. *Navajo: A Century of Progress, 1868–1968.* Window Rock, Ariz.: The Navajo Tribe, 1968.

Luckert, Karl W. *Coyoteway: A Navajo Holyway Healing Ceremonial.* Tucson: University of Arizona Press, 1979.

Matthews, Washington. *The Night Chant, a Navaho Ceremony* (Memoirs of the American Museum of Natural History, Vol. VI), New York, 1902 (*).

McNitt, Frank. *The Indian Traders.* Tucson: University of Oklahoma Press, 1979.

Mitchell, Frank. *Navajo Blessingway Singer. The Autobiography of Frank Mitchell, 1881–1967.* Edited by Charlotte J. Frisbie and David P. McAllester. Tucson: University of Arizona Press, 1978.

Newcomb, Franc J. *Hosteen Klah: Navaho Medicine Man and Sandpainter.* Norman: University of Oklahoma Press, 1964.

Parman, Donald L. *The Navajos and the New Deal.* New Haven, Conn.: Yale University Press, 1976.

Reichard, Gladys A. "Social Life of the Navajo Indians." *Columbia University Contributions to Anthropology* 7. New York, 1928.

———. *Navaho Religion: A Study of Symbolism.* 2 vols. New York: Pantheon Books, 1950.

Reno, Philip. *Mother Earth, Father Sky, and Economic Development: Navajo Resources and Their Use.* Albuquerque: University of New Mexico Press, 1981.

Roessel, Robert A. *Navajo History, 1850–1923.* HNAI 10: 506–523, 1983 (*).

Roessel, Ruth. *Women in Navajo Society.* Rough Rock, Ariz.: Navajo Curriculum Center, 1981.

———. *Navajo Arts and Crafts.* HNAI 10: 592–604, 1983 (*).

Roessel, Ruth, and Broderick H. Johnson, comps. *Navajo Livestock Reduction: A National Disgrace.* Tsaile, Ariz.: Navajo Community College Press, 1974.

Scudder, Thayer, et al. *No Place To Go: Effects of Compulsory Relocation on Navajos.* Philadelphia: Institute for the Study of Human Issues, 1982.

Shepardson, Mary. "Navajo Ways in Government: A Study in Political Process." *Memoirs of the American Association of Anthropology* 96. Menasha, Wisc., 1963.

———. *Development of the Navajo Tribal Government.* HNAI 10: 624–635, 1983 (*).

Thompson, Gerald E. *The Army and the Navajo: The Bosque Redondo Reservation Experiment, 1863–1868.* Tucson: University of Arizona Press, 1976.

Thompson, Hildegard. *The Navajos' Long Walk for Education.* Tsaile Lake, Ariz.: Navajo Community College Press, 1975.

Tome, Marshall. *The Navajo Nation Today.* HNAI 10: 679–683, 1983 (*).

Underhill, Ruth M. *The Navajos.* Norman: University of Oklahoma Press, 1956; 1967.

Williams, Aubrey W. "Navajo Political Process." *Smithsonian Contributions to Anthropology* 9. Washington, D.C., 1970.

Witherspoon, Gary. *Navajo Kinship and Marriage.* Chicago: University of Chicago Press, 1975 (*).

———. *Language and Art in the Navajo Universe.* Ann Arbor: University of Michigan Press, 1975.

———. *Navajo Social Organization.* HNAI 10: 524–535, 1983 (*).

Wyman, Leland C. *Blessingway.* Tucson: University of Arizona Press, 1970 (*).

———. *Navajo Ceremonial System.* HNAI 10: 536–557, 1983 (*).

INDEX

Italic page numbers indicate illustrations and captions.

A

Aberle, David F. 178, 202, 204
Adair, John 113
Agathla Peak (El Capitán) *20*
agriculture 30, 37–38, 45, 48, 75, 81–84, 108, 141, 202, 206 *See also* animal husbandry; *specific crop* (e.g., corn)
Agriculture, U.S. Department of 204
AIM (American Indian Movement) 202
Alaska 35
Albuquerque, New Mexico 75–76
alcoholism 179
alfalfa 83–84, *212, 216*
Anasazi 12–13, 36, *56, 132*
animal husbandry 39–40, 42–43, 73–81, 204, 206 *See also* cattle; donkeys; goats; horses; mules; sheep
animal life (in Navajo country) 14
Animas River 39
Apaches 35, 37, 42–43 *See also* Mescalero Apaches
Apaches de Nabajó 37–38, 84
apples 83
archaeology 38–39
Arizona 38, 50, 199, 206
Army, U.S. 115
Arts and Crafts Guild 114, 116
Arviso Jr., Tommy *230*
Assembly of God 179
Athapaskans 35–37, 40–41, 81
Atlantic and Pacific Railroad 76
automobiles *See* motor vehicles

B

Baptists 179
Barbas Güeras (Navajo leader) 142
Barboncito (Navajo leader) 46, 48, 142, *143*
barley 84
baskets and basketry 36, 39, 86, 115–116, *120*
bath, ritual 174
beans 82, 84, 174
Beauty Way Ceremony *192*
beef 78
Benavides, Alonso de 37
Betatakin (ancient settlement) *30, 56, 160*
BIA *See* Bureau of Indian Affairs
Big Mountain region 203
bilingual education 147, 197, 201, *226*
Black Mesa 50, 147, 202, 205, *210*
Blanca Peak 12
blankets 51, 73, 111, *124*
Blessing Way (*hózhójí*) 41, 171, 173–174
boarding schools 197, 198–199
Born for Water (mythical figure) 173
Bosque Redondo (Fort Sumner) 46, 48, *49, 58*, 73, 79, 82, 85, 111, 113, 141, 202, 204
bow and arrow 45
Brigham City, Utah 198
bronco riding *220*
bull-roarer *188*
Bureau of Indian Affairs (BIA)
administration by 48
economic policy 75, 78–80
employment by 207
political organizations 146–147
schools run by 197–200

C

Cabra Negra (Navajo leader) 142
California Column 46
Cambridge Ditch 83
Canada 35
cancer (from exposure to uranium) 205
Cañoncito 42
Canyon de Chelly 11, *30*, 42, 46, *56*, 82, *134*, 184
Canyon del Muerto *56, 58*
Carleton, James 46, *47*, 48
carpets *See* rugs and rug making
Carson, Christopher (Kit) 46, *47*
cattle 14, 40, 43, *58*, 73–74, 76, 78, 80–81, *92*, 138, 141–142, *216*
Cebolleta Mountains 39, 50
Central Plains 111
ceramics *See* pottery
ceremonial system 41, 115, 169–180, *184, 186, 188 See also* *specific ceremonies* (e.g., healing ceremonies)
CERT *See* Council of Energy Resources Tribes
Chaco Canyon 11, 13
Chacón, Don Fernando 40
Chaco Plateau 50
Chama Valley 37
Changing Woman 172–174
chants *See* songs and chants
"chapters" (self-help groups) 145–146, *166*
cheese 40
cherries 83
"chief's blankets" 111, *124*
children, responsibilities of *104*, 138
Chinle, Arizona 112, 199
Chinle Valley 50
Christianity 176 *See also* missions and missionaries; *spe-*